T0165184

BEAUTY AND THE BOTOX

A COLLECTION OF SHORT PLAYS

David J. Holcombe

authorHOUSE®

AuthorHouse™
1663 Liberty Drive
Bloomington, IN 47403
www.authorhouse.com
Phone: 1-800-839-8640

© 2011 David J. Holcombe. All rights reserved.

No part of this book may be reproduced, stored in a retrieval system, or transmitted by any means without the written permission of the author.

First published by AuthorHouse 10/7/2011

ISBN: 978-1-4670-2581-2 (sc)
ISBN: 978-1-4670-2514-0 (e)

Printed in the United States of America

Any people depicted in stock imagery provided by Thinkstock are models, and such images are being used for illustrative purposes only. Certain stock imagery © Thinkstock.

This book is printed on acid-free paper.

Because of the dynamic nature of the Internet, any web addresses or links contained in this book may have changed since publication and may no longer be valid. The views expressed in this work are solely those of the author and do not necessarily reflect the views of the publisher, and the publisher hereby disclaims any responsibility for them.

ACKNOWLEDGMENT &
DISCLAIMER

BEAUTY and the Botox, a Collection of Short Plays represents the culmination of many years of interest in play writing. At some point, it became obvious to me that the success of many well-crafted short stories often depended on the veracity and wit of the dialogue. Although a dialogue-driven plot offers some inconveniences, it also cuts to the chase of the tale and imposes restrictions of time and place that remove much of what might be considered superfluous.

Over the years, my personal fascination with the play format grew along with local participation and success in the Spectral Sisters Productions Ten Minute Play Festival. Being exposed to a number of visiting playwrights, including Doug Rand, Rosary O'Neill, Rachel Ladutke, Diane Glancey, Colin Denby Swanson and others, has helped nurture my interest and hone my skills. The result has been a number of local productions of some of my works in which "word becomes flesh," an astonishing and gratifying experience for any playwright. Putting on a play also enlists the participation of a whole host of directors, actors, set designers and technicians, each of whom add to the richness of the theatrical experience for the writer and the audience.

As in my previous short stories, the characters and events may have some resemblance to real circumstances and people. Any such associations are strictly fortuitous. I give thanks to those many people who have contributed to these plays, both as critics or possible characters, and especially to my long-suffering wife, who has put up with my literary pretentions over the years.

I would also like to acknowledge the contributions of Dr. Anton Chekhov, whose life and works have remained an inspiration to any aspiring physician-author. Dr. Chekhov never stopped practicing medicine, despite his prolific literary career. He felt his most enduring work was his scholarly study of the conditions in the Russian penal colony on Sakhalin Island. History has proved otherwise and we are all beneficiaries of his psychological insight and gift of language.

David J. Holcombe, MD
August 2011

Contents

ARRANGING THE SPICES

CAST OF CHARACTERS

MARIA: Young woman, Clara's daughter. She is dressed in causal, clean Eddie Bauer type clothing.

CLARA: An older woman, Maria's mother. She has her graying hair in a ponytail. She wears some flashy ethnic jewelry. She looks like an "old hippy." She is a retired English teacher and rather eccentric.

SETTING

There is a kitchen table with a couple of chairs. There is also a cabinet for spices, which also contains a few cook books. There are a dozen or more bottles of various spices scattered around.

(*MARIA watches as her mother, CLARA, arranges the spices by color. All of the bottles were scattered over the counter in total disarray. CLARA picks them up, one by one, and puts "order" into the chaos.*)

CLARA: You need to replace your spices every two years or even less to always have a fresh supply. (*Sniffs at some cinnamon.*) Let's put this cinnamon with the nutmeg and other brown spices, okay? (*Picks up another bottle.*) You know, dear, they lose their potency with time and they aren't that good for cooking, especially for entertaining.

MARIA: Mother, I really don't do that much entertaining anymore.

CLARA: (*Stops and stares at MARIA.*) Maybe that's why you're not already married and with children at your age. . . .

MARIA: (*Cuts CLARA off.*) I bet when you were my age, you didn't have massive genital warts either.

CLARA: (*Stops arranging the spices and looks at MARIA.*) You have what?

MARIA: (*Takes a bottle of spice from CLARA's hand and leads her to the kitchen table.*) I think you need to sit down for this.

CLARA: Is it so bad that I have to sit down?

MARIA: (*Shrugs.*) Maybe.

> (*CLARA wipes off the table with her hands before folding them in a position of thoughtful prayer.*)

MARIA: Mother, the table's not dirty. And I'm not contagious, unless you are having unprotected sex with me.

CLARA: That's disgusting. (*Pauses and narrows her eyes to slits.*) Go on. I'm listening.

MARIA: I have *condyloma accuminata*. That's Latin for genital warts. They look like small pink cauliflowers growing out of my vagina.

CLARA: (*Her face remains cold and immobile, devoid of emotion.*) How big?

> (*MARIA goes over and pulls out a photo, tucked between two cookbooks. She hands it to CLARA, who takes the edge with the tips of her fingers as if it, too, was infectious.*)

CLARA: (*Examines the photo.*) What is it?

MARIA: (*Turns the photo upside down and points to it.*) This is my vulva. And this is the top, with my pubic hair. And on the sides, you see all of this tissue. All those little fleshy bumps are genital warts.

CLARA: Who took this picture?

MARIA: (*Sighs.*) I asked the nurse practitioner at the health unit to take it so I could show you and anyone else who might be interested.

CLARA: It's horrible! How did you get these things?

MARIA: (*Takes the picture from between her mother's fingers and replaces it between the cookbooks. Returns to the table and sits down.*) It's a sexually transmitted disease, a virus. I think I got it from Greg. Or maybe it was Carl? Or Peter?

CLARA: (*Holds up her hand and cuts off MARIA.*) That's enough. Is it gone now? (*Resumes her prayerful position.*)

MARIA: No, it's not gone. It's just a bit less obvious. I could have gotten from any number of guys.

CLARA: So that's why you're not married?

(*MARIA does not answer.*)

CLARA: Can you still have children?

MARIA: Yes.

CLARA: (*Stands up and returns to the spices on the counter and continues her work.*) We need to get these spices in order. You can't live with this disorder. (*Pauses.*) And you have to get rid of those things, whatever they are and whoever gave them to you! How could you do such a thing?

MARIA: Mother, stop! You make me feel like I'm a child being scolded for a bad grade in English. I'm sexually active and financially independent and have been for years. And I still feel like the victim of your emotional blackmail. Can you just sit down so we can discuss this like adults?

CLARA: No! I want to get this in order first. How can you find anything in this cabinet? You need to have these all in order. Then we can see what you need and what has to be replaced. Spices are the cornerstone of good cooking.

MARIA: (*Stands up and removes the Hungarian Paprika from CLARA's hand.*) Don't you understand? I have enough spice in my life.

CLARA: (*Spins around.*) That's not funny! I always warned you, I never liked Greg. I bet he gave you this awful thing.

MARIA: (*Picks up a bottle.*) He did give me this dill. I don't know about the genital warts.

CLARA: (*Cringes and pushes a bottle away.*) Or Peter? Maybe he was the one. I didn't care for him either. He was a shifty character, with bad grammar.

MARIA: (*Picks up another bottle.*) And Carl? What about him. He gave me the saffron from Spain. Very expensive. Maybe he brought a little infection back with him?

CLARA: Well, Carl was okay, as long as he didn't give you these accumulated condylomas or whatever you call them.

(*CLARA ignores MARIA and resumes her work.*)

MARIA: Condyloma accuminata. (*Sighs.*) The point is that I can't say who gave me this problem. (*Puts down the bottle and goes over to the bookshelf and pulls out a little booklet.*) Do you know what this is?

CLARA: (*Looks over and shakes her head.*) No. It doesn't look familiar.

MARIA: (*Flips through the pages.*) It's my childhood vaccination booklet.

CLARA: (*Looks more closely.*) Yes, it is. I haven't seen that thing in years. What of it?

MARIA: (*Speaks loudly and firmly.*) Why didn't you let me get the HPV vaccination?

CLARA: (*Unscrews the bottle of dill and gives it a whiff.*) What?

MARIA: HPV.

CLARA: What is that?

MARIA: Human Papilloma Virus. It's sexually transmitted and it's the virus that causes genital warts. (*Pause.*) Mother, it's a preventable condition.

CLARA: (*Ignores MARIA and continues to sort the bottles.*) This basil looks moldy.

MARIA: Remember that vaccine? The one they offered when I was 11 or 12 years old?

CLARA: (*Pauses and looks lost in thought and then replaces the basil and takes a bottle of oregano.*) That was so many years ago. I do remember, vaguely.

MARIA: I remember like it was yesterday. You said you didn't want me to have that vaccine because it was experimental and chemical and would pollute my pre-adolescent body. And that I was too young and it would encourage me to have early sex. That's what you said, early sex.

CLARA: (*Sets the oregano down on the counter.*) How do you remember all that?

MARIA: I remember every word. I remember the nurse saying that it was safe and effective and not experimental and that it would protect me from cervical cancer and genital warts.

(*MARIA brings her fist down on the kitchen table.*)

MARIA: And now I have this shit and I can't get rid of it, ever! It's in me. It's in my cells. It grows and grows and it puts me at risk for cervical cancer.

CLARA: (*Replaces the bottle and comes over to the table. She places her hand gently on MARIA's shoulder*). Maria, please.

(*When CLARA's hand touches, her, MARIA shudders and pulls back. MARIA turns and looks into CLARA's eyes, barely a few inches away.*)

MARIA: Mother, I hate you!

CLARA: No! You can't hate your own mother.

MARIA: Yes! I hate you and your fake hippy naturalistic health crap. I hate you and your fresh spices and organic food and vegetarian bullshit.

CLARA: (*Pulls away.*) But it's important. Our bodies are a temple.

MARIA: Yes! And so is my vagina and now it doesn't look like a temple, it looks like a ruin filled with an alien cauliflower garden. And that stuff won't ever go away. Do you know how that makes me feel? (*Pauses.*) Mother, all I needed was three lousy shots and you didn't want them to give them to me. It's crazy.

CLARA: (*Comes over and sits beside MARIA at the table.*) I didn't know. I didn't understand that it was so important. For me, it was just dangerous chemicals in your body. I didn't want them to pollute your young, beautiful, pure body with an experimental vaccine that. . . . (*Her voice trails away.*)

MARIA: That promoted sexual promiscuity?

CLARA: Yes.

(*CLARA and MARIA sit in silence for a minute.*)

MARIA: So now I am sexually promiscuous anyway and I have a cauliflower vagina and I can get cervical cancer, too. Plus I have to warn any boyfriends that they can get this stuff on their dicks. So they have to wear condoms to protect themselves. It's so romantic.

(MARIA *looks over at her mother, who sits upright, with her hands again folded in a prayer-like position. MARIA gets up and goes behind CLARA, who remains rigid and motionless. MARIA slides her hands over CLARA's and they come to rest around CLARA's interlaced fingers.*)

MARIA: I know you meant well. But you were wrong and I'm paying the price for the rest of my life.

CLARA: (*Turns her head and reveals her tear-filled eyes.*) Maria, I'm so sorry. I was foolish. I didn't understand. (*Pauses.*) But I didn't make you sleep with all those men. I didn't make you have unprotected sex. Don't you have to accept any responsibility for your own actions? (*Clutches MARIA's hand.*) Aren't we both to blame here just a little?

MARIA: All your talk about Woodstock and Free Love. I believed you. I really did. Did you really believe any of that? What were your consequences?

CLARA: I did believe in Free Love. And I was lucky enough not to get genital warts. (*Pauses.*) I got you. And I would not trade you for all the spices in world. I love you, warts and all. Please forgive me. (*Walks over and embraces MARIA.*)

MARIA: (*Kisses CLARA and then pulls away and sighs.*) I guess I am better than genital warts. But I still have to live with this nightmare and you can go on with your macrobiotic food and solar panels. You can shop at Whole Foods and eat organic vegetables in peace.

CLARA: How can I be in peace knowing that my own flesh and blood suffers? (*Pauses.*) Can I make it up to you somehow?

MARIA: (*Releases CLARA's hands.*) Finish arranging the spices. (*Picks up a bottle off the counter and hands it to CLARA.*) And please do it alphabetically and not by color. Here's the curry. It goes after the cumin. I think Peter gave me that one.

THE END

ARTISTIC INTEGRITY

CAST OF CHARACTERS

ARTURO: A middle aged artist, dressed in working clothes, splashed with paint.

NANCY: Arturo's wife. She is also middle aged and casually dressed.

HENRIETTA MANSFIELD: She can be middle aged or older. She is elegantly dressed in matching pants suit and jacket, with a blouse and color coordinated scarf. She wears flashy designer jewelry. She has an affected way of speaking, with exaggerated emphasis on certain words.

SETTING

This is the artist's studio. There is an easel with a painting, which has its back to the audience. There is a small table with a paint palette and enough space for a tray with a pitcher and a couple of glasses. Everyone stands, so no chairs are necessary.

(*ARTURO places bold splashes of paint on the canvas. Since the audience only sees the back of the painting, no actual paint is necessary, just some large brushes. NANCY enters from backstage and looks at the painting without him being aware. She is holding a tray with a pitcher of lemonade and a couple of glasses.*)

NANCY: That's beautiful. As you say yourself, sometimes the magic's there and sometimes it's not. Well, I think this time the magic's definitely there.

ARTURO: (*Smiles and turns to NANCY.*) Thanks.

NANCY: (*Deposits the tray with two glasses and a pitcher of lemonade on a space next to his palette.*) I thought you might like a little refreshment after a hard morning's work.

ARTURO: (*Sets down the brush and picks up a glass.*) To my muse! Thanks for the help.

NANCY: Behind every successful man is a successful woman, isn't that what they say?

ARTURO: Yes, they do.

NANCY: (*Examines the painting.*) This is good, really good. Who's it for?

ARTURO: I promised Henrietta Mansfield I'd donate something for their art auction for the homeless shelter later this week. You know how persistent she can be. Besides, it's for a good cause.

NANCY: (*Sets her glass down on the tray with a trembling hand.*) Not that woman again! She's already asked you for a painting for their silent auction for the last three years. If you keep giving your art away instead of selling it, we're going to be homeless. And do you think Mrs. Mansfield is going to give us some money for our overdue mortgage?

ARTURO: (*Turns back to face the canvas and picks up a brush to resume painting.*) Don't exaggerate! It is a good cause and we are not homeless.

NANCY: Yet! We have to pay our home insurance, our health insurance, the car payment, the 401K contribution, what little there is in it, and of course we have to eat unless you think we can do without that, too.

ARTURO: Nancy, you're not being reasonable. This is a fairly small work and you know they count on all the community artists to contribute to the silent auction.

NANCY: Yes, all the starving artists. I know what they do. Mrs. Mansfield and her rich do-gooder cronies rely on the people like you with the least money and expect them to donate so rich people can get artwork for half price! (*Swings her hands around in the air.*) What kind of a stupid exploitative system is that?

ARTURO: God has given me this talent and I can only pass it on with the same celestial generosity. (*Pauses.*) Remember Khalil Gibran's immortal words, "You say you would give, but only to the deserving. The flocks in your field say not so, nor the trees in your orchards, for to withhold is to perish." (*Lowers his head in a dramatic gesture of submission to higher powers.*)

NANCY: (*Laughs a long raucous, irritating laugh.*) To withhold is to perish, eh? Well, to withhold is also to sell for a thousand bucks or more to someone out of the gallery in Dallas. Wouldn't that make more sense than letting someone buy your painting for three hundred dollars at that stupid auction for the homeless? Oh yes, and I forgot, out of that three hundred, half goes to pay the cost of the event and maybe the other half goes to the homeless shelter. (*Pauses.*) Not only that, but if we don't pay your life insurance premium and you happen to die on me, I really would be out on the street with nothing. (*Pauses.*) Please just send that painting to the gallery and get a decent price. Then you can give 10% to the poor or whatever you want to.

ARTURO: There's no guarantee I'd sell in Dallas.

NANCY: Yeah, but there is a guarantee that you won't get anything by giving it away to Mrs. Mansfield. (*Pauses.*) Except perhaps a place in heaven.

(*NANCY shakes her head while ARTURO continues to apply paint to the canvas.*)

NANCY: Please listen to me. This is a wonderful work. It's a stroke of genius. You are a brilliant artist and I adore you and what you do. But you can be so blind sometimes.

ARTURO: (*Stops painting.*) You're spoiling my artistic mood. You are interfering with my artistic genius. (*Slams down the brush and swings to face NANCY.*) And how can I be a visual genius and be blind at the same time? Tell me that if you're so smart, eh?

NANCY: (*Softens and pours more lemonade.*) I don't know. Those contradictions are part of your mystique and your irresistible attraction. (*Examines the painting.*) Just look at those strokes, so full of passion and surprise. None of those cheapskate rich bastards can recognize the genius of your works. (*Pauses.*) Give them something else, some sketch or other paper work. Anything but this! This is unadulterated beauty. This deserves a good home. (*Pauses.*) At a decent price.

ARTURO: Price! Money! Materialism! That's all you think about. How can you expect me to give anything but my best? To do any less would be a travesty, a personal sacrifice, a betrayal of artistic integrity. I can't give some second-rate product, some worthless sketch. It's my best or nothing at all!

NANCY: (*Moves some brushes around and begins dusting off the edge of his work table.*) How dirty it gets in here.

ARTURO: Stop that! We are having an important discussion about art and charity and personal integrity and you're cleaning up like some brainless maid.

(*NANCY stops and sets down the brush. She is obviously wounded.*)

ARTURO: I'm sorry. I didn't mean that.

NANCY: Didn't you?

ARTURO: No. I didn't mean it. I respect you and love you for everything you do. (*Sets down the brush and goes over and gives NANCY a hug.*) You are my best critic, my muse, my best friend and my lover. What more could I ask for?

NANCY: So you'll give something else besides this painting to Mrs. Mansfield?

ARTURO: (*Unclasps his arms and returns to his work.*) NO! It's a matter of principle.

(*NANCY opens her mouth, and then shuts it again as the doorbell rings.*)

NANCY: I'll get that.

(*HENRIETTA MANSFIELD, dressed in an elegant beige pant suit and matching scarf, sweeps into the room. She makes large, dramatic gestures.*)

HENRIETTA: You must be Arturo's wife, Nancy. Such a pleasure to meet you at last. (*Crosses the room, passing by NANCY, and gives ARTURO an air kiss on each cheek.*) Am I interrupting something?

NANCY: Yes.

ARTURO: No, of course not. (*Pauses.*) To what do we owe the pleasure of your visit?

HENRIETTA: (*Moves around to examine the work of art.*) Oh, I'm just flitting around checking on all the donating artists to see how they are doing. (*Leans forward and scrutinizes the painting from just a few inches away.*) Very nice, Arturo. Very nice, indeed. It's so full of passion and visual intensity, with a touch of moody anger if I'm not mistaken. (*Looks from ARTURO to his NANCY.*) Are you sure I'm not interrupting something?

NANCY: Yes.

ARTURO: Of course not! (*Motions to the tray with the pitcher and turns toward NANCY.*) Perhaps Mrs. Mansfield would like a drink of lemonade?

HENRIETTA: That would be lovely. It's not an imposition, is it?

ARTURO: Of course not.

NANCY: (*Scowling with anger.*) I'll be right back with another glass. (*Exits the stage.*)

HENRIETTA: (*Steps back from the canvas and examines it from a distance, approaches and almost puts her face in it.*) This is really stunning. Have you finished it yet?

ARTURO: Yes, I just put the last touches on recently.

HENRIETTA: So it's ready?

ARTURO: I guess so. Do you need it right now?

HENRIETTA: I'd love to take it home with me. (*Takes the painting and looks at it.*) Amazing.

NANCY: (*Enters the room with the lemonade.*) Here's your lemonade. (*Sees HENRIETTA holding the painting.*) Leaving so soon?

HENRIETTA: Oh yes. I've just got to see how this looks in the natural light. It's a masterpiece.

NANCY: (*Hands HENRIETTA a rag.*) You might want something to clean your hands.

HENRIETTA: (*Puts the painting back and looks at her dirty hands.*) It's still wet! Look at my hands! It's going to get onto my dress. (*Snatches the rag and begins cleaning her hands.*)

NANCY: Some lemonade? Or would you prefer some turpentine. . .for your hands, of course.

HENRIETTA: (*Throws the rag on the table and looks at the painting. To ARTURO.*) Do you think it will be dry by this weekend for the auction?

ARTURO: (*Looks at HENRIETTA and back to the painting.*) I've been so busy lately that I just finished it today. (*Pauses.*) I'm afraid, there's no way this will be dry by the end of the week, especially with these thick layers of pigment. I'm really sorry, but I just may not be able to donate anything this year.

HENRIETTA: (*Scans the studio, looking for some other works of art.*) Don't you have anything else ready?

ARTURO: No, everything else is tied up in a show in Dallas. And that's not over for six weeks. I'm very sorry. You know I'm a man of my word, but I can't give you a wet piece of art. Maybe next year.

NANCY: (*Offers HENRIETTA a glass of lemonade.*) Are you sure you don't want a glass?

HENRIETTA: Oh, no thank you, dear. (*Holds up her hand to stop NANCY.*) I'm just too disappointed to enjoy lemonade. Your husband's beautiful work will not be ready for the homeless shelter auction. Such a tragedy. Just yesterday, I went to the shelter to hand out fresh linens. To see those poor men, it just broke my heart. It's so deplorable.

NANCY: (*To ARTURO.*) Yes, that's such a pity, isn't it dear? (*To HENRIETTA.*) You must be so disappointed, Mrs. Mansfield.

HENRIETTA: Yes, I'm crushed. Each dollar we raise helps those poor hopeless souls, plus I so wanted another one of Arturo's works. I've been able to get one of his masterpieces for half price for the last three years. (*Pauses and points to the canvas.*) And this one would have been perfect with the others in my atrium.

(*ARTURO stares at NANCY.*)

HENRIETTA: I guess I'll just have to wait until next year. (*Turns and walks toward the door.*) So nice to meet you at last, Nancy. Perhaps you'll both be attending the auction this weekend? It's only $50 a ticket and I'm sure you'll enjoy the food and the music. I'd offer you some complimentary tickets, but those are only available to artists who plan on donating something to the auction.

ARTURO: No, Mrs. Mansfield, my wife and I have a previous engagement. I'll be sure to send in a check to the cause.

> (*ARTURO watches HENRIETTA walk out off stage as NANCY refills their glasses with lemonade. NANCY hands ARTURO a glass.*)

NANCY: To artistic integrity!

ARTURO: (*Clinks glasses.*) Yes, to artistic integrity!

THE END

BEAUTY AND THE BOTOX

CAST OF CHARACTERS

VIVIAN RILEY: Middle aged woman who has begun to look her age. She is very well dressed.

DR. FARRIS: Plastic surgeon with a specialty in Botox treatments. He is dressed in a white lab coat over a colored shirt and tie. He wears slacks and polished shoes.

AUTHOR'S NOTE

This should be played as a black comedy. The actors should give over-the-top interpretations, which allow the audience to absorb the somber message while laughing at the characters. The music used can be "You're so Vain," by Carly Simon (1972).

SETTING

The stage is divided into three areas by pools of light. On stage right is a pool of light with Vivian at her make-up table. The center pool of light is on a table, which will serve as an operating table in the surgical suite. On stage left is Dr. Farris's office with a desk, covered with papers and vials, and a lamp.

VIVIAN: (*Looks at the mirror and speaks to herself.*) Look at those hideous wrinkles around my mouth and eyes. (*Sighs.*) All of these ugly reminders of age need to disappear. Why suffer the indignities of age when modern medicine offers all the necessary solutions? (*Holds up a full-page, color ad and examines it closely.*) Look at these women. Look at these ugly hags before Botox injections and look at them afterwards. Shriveled sixty-year-old women become thirty-something beauties. Of course make-up and lighting enhance the results, but, all in all, the changes are impressive, much too impressive to pass up. (*Picks her cell phone and dials.*) Hello. Is this the Complete Cosmetic Care Clinic? (*Pauses.*) This is Vivian Riley. I'd like some prices on Botox injections, please. (*Pauses.*) Yes, around the eyes and the mouth for starters. How much would that cost? (*Pauses.*) Three thousand dollars! (*Pauses.*) Of course I realize that my insurance company will not cover the cost of Botox treatments. (*Pauses.*) I'll take the appointment with Dr. Farris on Thursday at 2:30, but can't I come in any earlier? I want to have this done before my high school reunion next week. (*Listens.*) You have a cancellation this afternoon. Yes, that would be wonderful. The sooner, the better. (*Continues getting dressed and examines herself in the mirror.*) Dr. Farris will make me young and beautiful again. Thank God for Dr. Farris.

(*The light dims on VIVIAN and go up on DR. FARRIS in his office. He is speaking into his cell phone.*)

DR. FARRIS: That damned GenetoQuest stock has plunged from 86 dollars a share to only two dollars. That's practically junk stock level. (*Pauses.*) You swore to me GenetoQuest was supposed to be the latest, hottest pick in the market. Now I've lost a bundle. I'd be selling off shares for a miserable pittance of what I'd paid a few months ago. (*Pauses.*) Yes, I can deduct some capital losses from my taxes, but that doesn't help me pay the office staff, my mortgages, my malpractice insurance and those damn supply costs. (*Pauses.*) No! I'm not in the mood to invest in anything more at the moment and certainly not in GenetoQuest. Goodbye!

(*DR. FARRIS slams his phone shut and stuffs it in his pocket. Then he picks up a vial of Botox and examines it.*)

DR. FARRIS: You'd think that this stuff was gold. Over $50,000 for a box of vials of this precious substance. Sure, it helps me make a bundle, but $50,000 for every box of vials! That's highway robbery. (*Examines the bottle.*) I should have listened to Edward. I could have joined his practice in Los Angeles and done 60 boobs a month, a different starlet every day. (*Picks up the vial and holds it to the light.*) It looks like water, plain ordinary tap water. (*Pauses.*) If I could figure out some way to dilute it and still retain its effectiveness, I could do two or three more patients with each bottle. I could double my profit margin for every single patient. Now that would be a decent return on my investment.

(VIVIAN knocks at the door. DR. FARRIS places the bottle on the desk. VIVIAN enters.)

VIVIAN: Hello. I'm Vivian Riley.

DR. FARRIS: *(Stands up to greet her.)* Good afternoon. I'm Dr. Farris. Nice to meet you. Please sit down. *(Indicates a chair.)* What can we do for you today, Mrs. Riley?

VIVIAN: *(Sits.)* First, call me Vivian. Second, I'd like to have these crow's feet removed from around my eyes and mouth, doctor. You see them. *(Leans forward.)*

DR. FARRIS: *(Bends forward and studies her face, glances at her neck, arms and thighs, and finally lifts up one of her breasts and jiggles it a little.)* I'm afraid there's a bit more here than just a face job.

VIVIAN: I know, doctor. There's a lot more to do, but I just need the face done before next week.

DR. FARRIS: A cruise?

VIVIAN: No. A class reunion.

DR. FARRIS: *(Touches her face and pulls the skin taut.)* I see. Yes, Vivian. I think we can help you. Your mouth and eyes will look twenty years younger. I can make you the most beautiful woman in the buffet line. *(Walks behind his desk and pulls out a few papers on a clip board.)* You do understand that insurance companies do not reimburse cosmetic surgeries or Botox injections?

VIVIAN: Of course.

DR. FARRIS: And you also understand the results may vary from patient to patient?

VIVIAN: Of course.

DR. FARRIS: (*Picks up her chart and makes some notations.*) We can do the eyes and mouth, and perhaps some areas of the chin and forehead. The effects should last at least two or three months, more than enough time for your class reunion.

VIVIAN: Only two to three months? For three thousand dollars?

DR. FARRIS: Yes. This is not surgery, just a temporary treatment. And Botox is extremely expensive, a thousand dollars for a little bottle. (*Shows her a vial and then sets it down.*) We could consider some more definitive surgical procedures later if you're pleased with the results.

VIVIAN: It would be nice to get some definitive therapy, but we'll just go ahead with the Botox for now. The sooner the better.

DR. FARRIS: Good. We just happen to have an opening today. (*Passes her a series of papers to sign.*) This is a consent form for the procedure, just a precaution, of course. And this is a statement which declares that you understand this procedure will not be reimbursed by your insurance.

(*VIVIAN glances at the papers and signs.*)

DR. FARRIS: If you can just go across into the operating room, I'll be along in a few moments.

VIVIAN: Thank you, doctor.

(*VIVIAN exits to center stage and gets into a hospital gown. VIVIAN climbs onto the table, sits on the edge, and waits. The lights dim and go back onto DR. FARRIS in his office.*)

DR. FARRIS: (*Pulls out a number of bottles and syringes in order to adulterate the Botox.*) Lidocaine might work for diluting the Botox, but it could result in more rapid absorption and the cosmetic results might fade too fast. (*Holds another vial up.*) Glycerin's a possibility, but it's so thick it might clog the needle and cause too much pain at the injection site. (*Holds up a third bottle.*) Plasmanate seems like a good choice, not too thick, but that damn stuff's almost as expensive as Botox. Why bother using something as expensive as the original? (*Plays with the bottles.*) A combination of glycogen and lidocaine might be perfect, not too thick, not too irritating, and not too expensive. (*Fills a syringe with the combination.*) Now, just to be on the safe side, let's try a little self injection test. After all, **primum non nocere,** first do no harm. (*Eases the needle into his forearm and winces a little from the pain.*) A little painful, but I guess that would just prove I'm injecting something. No pain. No gain. (*Rubs his arm at the site of the injection and then he holds up the bottle.*) Yes, this is my ticket to substantial overhead savings. At a two to one dilution, I can save about $50,000 a week in Botox costs. That should at least cover some of my losses from the GenetoQuest fiasco.

(*DR. FARRIS takes off his white coat and dons a green surgical smock and hat. He goes across to the operating table upon which VIVIAN is sitting. DR. FARRIS takes a clipboard and begins to make some notations.*)

DR. FARRIS: Mrs. Vivian Riley, correct?

VIVIAN: Yes. My name hasn't changed in the last five minutes.

DR. FARRIS: Of course. It's just a formality. (*Appears irritated at her remark and makes a notation.*) And we're doing bilateral peri-orbital and peri-buccal Botox injections?

VIVIAN: I guess that means around the eyes and mouth, doctor?

DR. FARRIS: Yes. It certainly does. Sorry about the medical gibberish. (*Looks irritated and makes an angry check make in the chart.*) How are you feeling today?

VIVIAN: Fine, Dr. Farris. Just a little nervous.

DR. FARRIS: That's perfectly normal. This is your first time, isn't it?

VIVIAN: Yes.

DR. FARRIS: It will be just fine. You'll see. Any allergies?

VIVIAN: Nothing but eggs.

DR. FARRIS: Eggs? (*Pauses and looks from the chart up at VIVIAN.*) How allergic?

VIVIAN: Oh, pretty allergic. I swell up like a balloon if I eat them. But I'm very careful. And I haven't had a reaction in years. Maybe I grew out of it?

DR. FARRIS: (*Pauses a long time and looks back and forth at VIVIAN and the chart.*) Eggs, eh?

VIVIAN: Is there a problem, doctor?

DR. FARRIS: No. No. I'm just getting your paperwork in order. Not allergic to any drugs?

VIVIAN: No.

DR. FARRIS: (*Laughs a nervous laugh.*) No drug allergies. Good. Eggs aren't drugs. Why complicate matters with a little detail like that? (*Puts the file on the stainless steel counter and pushes a portable table, loaded with various syringes and vials toward the patient.*) Okay, Vivian. Let's make you young again.

(*The lights come on with greater intensity on VIVIAN and DR. FARRIS.*)

DR. FARRIS: Just close your eyes. Ready?

VIVIAN: Yes, doctor. I'm ready. I'm ready to see the looks of surprise and envy when I stride into the gymnasium at my high school reunion. No one will understand how I have escaped the ravages of time. I want be the queen of the prom again, the most beautiful, the most elegant girl at Brasher High School. I want to be a vision of youth. Go ahead. (*Lies down on the table.*)

27

DR. FARRIS: (*Drapes her in a blue surgical sheet so only her face is exposed.*) Okay. Now here we go around the eyes. (*Injects around the right eye.*)

VIVIAN: Ouch! That really hurts!

DR. FARRIS: That's the Botox going in. It does sting a little.

VIVIAN: A little? That really hurts.

DR. FARRIS: Well, some people do feel it more than others. (*Pokes around the eyes some more.*) A touch here. A touch there. Away go the wrinkles. Away go the years. (*Moves across to the left side, injecting multiple times around the left eye before starting around the mouth on the left side.*) Now, let's restore that beautiful smile.

VIVIAN: Doctor, am I supposed to feel chest tightness?

DR. FARRIS: Sometimes a little, but it goes away quickly.

VIVIAN: (*Begins to pant in short non-productive bursts and clutch her chest with both hands.*) Doctor, I can't breathe.

DR. FARRIS: We're almost done, Vivian. Just a few more touches on the right. Take slow, deep breaths. Some people do get a little anxious the first time.

VIVIAN: (*Continues to pant with a rasping breath, like a death rattle.*) Doctor, I'm frightened. (*Gasps.*) I can't breathe! I really can't breathe! (*Clutches her throat and goes limp.*)

DR. FARRIS: (*Ignores her and continues poking.*) There! All done. (*Pulls back the sterile cloth that covered most of VIVIAN's face.*) You should look years younger. (*Bends forward to examine his work and looks more closely at VIVIAN's face.*) Vivian! Mrs. Riley! Are you all right?

(*VIVIAN makes a final guttural sound and twitches in a last post mortem spasm. DR. FARRIS watches in horror as VIVIAN twitches. DR. FARRIS, clutches her shoulders and shakes VIVIAN violently.*)

DR. FARRIS: Vivan! Wake up!

(*VIVIAN stops twitching and goes limp.*)

DR. FARRIS: Oh my God! (*Looks around in desperation.*) Nurse! Nurse!

(*No one comes in. DR. FARRIS is panicking. He bends forward and pinches VIVIAN's nose and applies his own lips to hers. DR. FARRIS breathes in a couple of times. Nothing happens. DR. FARRIS backs away.*)

DR. FARRIS: My God, she's dying. (*Feels VIVIAN's neck.*) No pulse. Oh shit! Was it two breaths and two compressions or five compressions and one breath? (*Places his hands over her chest and plunges in.*) One, two, three, four, five. (*Breathes into her mouth.*) One, two. (*Feels her neck.*) No pulse. (*Replaces his hands on the chest.*) One, two, three, four, five. (*Feels her neck again.*) Nothing. No breathing. No pulse. She can't die. Not here. Not now. (*Applies his lips to hers.*) Nothing. (*Compresses a few more times.*) Nothing. (*Backs away and pulls out his cell phone.*) 911. Yes, this is Dr. Farris. I have a patient in cardiac arrest here at the clinic. (*Pauses.*) Yes, 1714 Natchitoches Drive, Fulton. Send an ambulance STAT! (*Puts his phone back in his pocket and stares at VIVIAN's limp form. Then he looks at the bottle of Botox. He snatches it up and looks at it.*) I gotta get rid of this. (*Grabs the syringe as well.*) They'll find this stuff. They'll analyze it. I'll go to prison. I'll get the electric chair. I'll lose my license. (*Stares wildly around the room.*) They can't find this. (*Rushes around and finally comes back to Vivian's side. Loads up the syringe with the remaining adulterated Botox and manages, with difficulty, to inject himself with the rest of the vial.*) Now rinse it out with saline. Rinse it out. (*Fumbles with bottles while cluthing his arm.*) God! This burns like hell. I can't believe this. (*Starts to hyperventilate. Clutches his chest and falls against VIVIAN.*)

I must've hit a vein. (*Looks down at VIVIAN.*) You vain bitch! You're killing me. I'm dying. Christ! I'm dying. (*Looks around in panic.*) I gotta get some epinephrine.

(*DR. FARRIS goes to his desk where he rummages through the drawers.*)

DR. FARRIS: Where's that stuff. My God. I gotta get that epinephrine. (*Clutches a bunch of papers that he crumples in his hand and throws down.*) Genetoquest stock! Where's that epinephrine? (*Continues to look and finally pulls out another bottle.*) There it is.

(*DR. FARRIS pulls out a bottle and injects himself with what he thinks is epinephrine. DR. FARRIS looks a little more relaxed until he studies the bottle and reacts with horror.*)

DR. FARRIS: Botox!

(*DR. FARRIS drops the bottle and wipes the remaining papers off the desk as he collapses to the floor in front of the desk. There, he clutches his chest, gasps, and starts a raspy death rattle. He twitches a little on the floor, then lies still, obviously dead. The sound of an ambulance gets louder and louder as the lights dim to dark on the two corpses.*)

THE END

COONS FOR SALE

CAST OF CHARACTERS

BRUCE MAYNARD: He is a young to middle aged man, dressed in jeans and a bulky hunter's or GI jacket. He speaks with a rural Louisiana accent. He is wearing a large hunting knife as well.

THOMAS DUPONT: He is also a young to middle aged man, dressed in a button-down shirt and slacks. He is wearing a badge from the Louisiana Office of Public Health. He may have a slight Cajun accent, but not overwhelming.

PETER MANSFIELD: He is an older man, with shaggy hair and a beard. He is dressed in a flannel shirt and overalls or other country apparel. He also has a pronounced rural accent. He wears a prominent holster and firearm.

SERGEANT PHILLIP COSTER: He is dressed in a police uniform. He wears a side-arm and the other usual police accoutrements, including a taser.

SETTING

An impromptu stand by the side of the road in a winter afternoon.

(BRUCE is sitting in a folding chair. Beside him is a big cardboard box, refrigerator size. "COONS FOR SALE" is printed in large unequal letter in red or black paint. He is whittling a piece of wood with his hunting knife. THOMAS DUPONT comes up to confront BRUCE about his coon stand.)

THOMAS: Are those your coons?

BRUCE: Sure are. Best damn coons in all of Tunica Parish. Fat, juicy and ready to roast.

THOMAS: Can I see one?

(*BRUCE puts his knife away and reaches into the box and pulls out a large, clear plastic bag with a bloody raccoon carcass. It is the size of a small dog. One of the black paws is prominently displayed.*)

BRUCE: Look at this baby. It must be a twelve pounder. (*Points to the paw.*) And you see, there's the paw to prove this is the real thing. Not some dog, like other people around here tries to do. I sell a good, clean product. This baby'll only cost you ten bucks and that's a real bargain. Cheaper than turkey and twice as good.

(*THOMAS takes the bag and examines it closely. Then he hands it back to BRUCE.*)

THOMAS: You can't sell raccoon meat.

BRUCE: What do you mean, I can't sell coon meat. I've been doin' it in this parts for years now. I got regular happy return customers. They wait all year just to buy 'em a fat coon for Christmas.

THOMAS: I'm sorry. You can't sell raccoon meat.

BRUCE: Who says?

THOMAS: (*Points to his Office of Public Health badge.*) I say. I'm Tommy Dupont and I work for the Louisiana Office of Public Health and I'm shutting down your coon sales.

BRUCE: You can't do that. I killed these coons all summer and now I got fifteen of them left. You can't shut me down like that.

THOMAS: I sure can. And I'm goin' confiscate your coons so you don't sell 'em tomorrow someplace else.

BRUCE: But somebody from Wildlife and Fisheries told me it was okay to kill 'em and sell 'em. And I got me a peddler's permit from the city. Look at it!

(BRUCE presents a piece of paper from his jacket pocket. THOMAS examines it and gives it back to BRUCE.)

THOMAS: They were mistaken. You can kill coons, you can eat coons, but you can't sell 'em to people, even if you have a permit from the city.

(THOMAS begins to pull the whole box off stage left. PETER MANSFIELD walks up and assesses the situation.)

PETER: Hello Bruce. You got any Christmas coons left. I need one for the family.

BRUCE: Yeah, Pete. I had fifteen of 'em left. But I ain't got none left now.

PETER: What's the matter?

BRUCE: Mr. Dupont here from the Health Department is goin' confiscate my coons as a public danger. He says I can't sell coons. It's illegal.

PETER: *(To THOMAS.)* What you mean he can't sell his coons?

THOMAS: That's right. You can't sell coon in Louisiana unless it's been slaughtered at a licensed processing plant. And there aren't any in the State of Louisiana, or anyplace else for that matter. There's no way to tell how these animals have been prepared or under what conditions. I gotta shut down this man's operation and I'm goin' have to confiscate his coons.

PETER: *(To BRUCE.)* You goin' let this government asshole take your property like that?

BRUCE: What am I supposed to do?

PETER: You got your knife, ain't you?

BRUCE: Sure. I always carry one.

PETER: And I got better than that. (*Shows his sidearm.*)

THOMAS: (*Stops pulling at the box when he sees the gun and backs away.*) Hey boys. I'm not interested in any fighting. I'm not armed and I'm not dangerous. (*To Peter*) So maybe you ought to just back away and go on home.

PETER: I ain't goin' home. And I suggest you better leave them coons just like you found 'em and let Mr. Bruce here go about his business.

THOMAS: He can't sell coons. It's a violation of the sanitary code. That means it's against the law.

PETER: (*Threatening THOMAS with the gun.*) You little bureaucratic asshole! You think because you work for the Office of Public Health you can go around terrorizing God-fearing, hard-working folks just trying to make them a livin'? You think this is Communist China or Russia or someplace like that? We got rights, mister! We got a right to shoot coons and shoot Communist bureaucrats who come and take away our rights. Ain't that so, Bruce?

BRUCE: (*Nods weakly.*) Pete, don't go threatenin' that guy. He's just trying to do his job.

PETER: Doin' his job! He's supposed to be workin' for us. He's a God-damned public servant. We pay this man with our taxes. And I say he's not doin' his job. (*To BRUCE.*) Why don't you go and shut down some of those guys sellin' dope to the kids down off Parliament Street, eh? (*Swings his gun around as he speaks.*) Yeah, go down there and terrorizes some real criminals selling somethin' really bad to people instead of botherin' honest country folks tryin' to make an honest livin'.

(*SERGEANT PHILLIP COSTER comes in from stage left. He is looking at THOMAS, the box of coons, BRUCE and PETER. His eyes follow PETER's gun as it swings around the air. He ends up speaking to THOMAS.*)

35

SERGEANT: Hello, Tom. What the hell is goin' on here?

THOMAS: I'm tryin' to shut down the illegal coon sales.

SERGEANT: And this guy? (*To PETER.*) Hey, mister, don't you be swingin' a firearm around like that. You got a permit for that pistol?

PETER: I sure as hell do! I got a permit for this baby and a lot more like it at home, too. You wanna see my assault rifle?

SERGEANT: Mister, why don't you put that pistol away and let this man do his job.

PETER: (*Screaming.*) Job! Do his job! This is how it starts. (*To BRUCE.*) Don't you see. First they take away your coons. Then they take away your guns. Then they take away your wife and children. Don't you see! It's a left-wing liberal Communist plot and we gotta draw the line somewhere. Bruce, pull out that knife and help me!

SERGEANT: Calm down, mister. Give me that gun and I'll check to see if it's registered. I gotta do that. (*To BRUCE.*) And why don't you give me that knife while you're at it.

BRUCE: I don't need a permit for hunting knife, do I?

SERGEANT: No. I just don't like the look of it right at this minute.

> (*BRUCE begins to hand the knife, handle first, to SERGEANT COSTER. PETER rushes over and pushes BRUCE's arm away. The knife falls to the ground.*)

PETER: Don't do it, man! Don't give up that knife. We gotta take a stand somewhere and this is a good a spot as any.

THOMAS: At a coon stand? You gotta be kidding. (*To BRUCE.*) Keep the damned coons if you want. I'd just have to figure out a way to get rid of 'em anyway.

BRUCE: You mean you would just dump 'em?

THOMAS: Well, actually we pour bleach on 'em, first so nobody goes in the dumpster to retrieve 'em.

BRUCE: That's a terrible waste, a real crime.

THOMAS: That's what I'm tellin' you. Just take the coons away. Give 'em to your friends and family. Eat 'em yourself. Just don't sell 'em on the street. It's not safe and it's not legal.

PETER: It's not about the coon, man! (*To BRUCE.*) It's about abuse of authority. It's about preserving our God given personal freedoms preserved in the Constitution of the United States of America. (*Swings the gun around and points to THOMAS and SERGEANT COSTER.*) It's about you two Fascist Communist bastards trying to get my coon (*Grabs the coon and waves the bag around*) and my gun!

BRUCE: Pete, just let the officer check the registration for your gun. It's no big deal. You can have the coon if you want. It's a gift, from me to you.

PETER: Yes, it's a big deal. (*Stands on the folding chair and continues to swing the raccoon carcass and pistol.*) You will have to pry this coon and this gun out of my cold, dead fingers!

> (*PETER points the gun at the three others, who duck behind the coon box. SERGEANT COSTER pokes his head about the edge.*)

SERGEANT: Gimme that gun, mister! Now!

PETER: NEVER!

SERGEANT: (*On his radio.*) Please send some back up down to the corner of Fulton and Evergreen Street. I gotta an armed crazy.

PETER: (*To BRUCE, who is poking his head up.*) Pick up that knife and stab him! Bruce, stab 'em both. You're right there. It's our moment of victory. I can smell it.

(*BRUCE shakes his head and ducks back behind the box. THOMAS yells out to PETER.*)

THOMAS: That's coon carcass you smell, you old fool!

PETER: Okay. If I'm on my own, I'm on my own. Give me liberty or give me death!

(*PETER points the gun in the direction of the box. SERGEANT COSTER pops up and shoots PETER with a taser. PETER goes into a shaking fit and falls to the ground. The coon and the gun fall, too. SERGEANT COSTER goes over and picks up the gun. THOMAS goes over and picks up the bloody coon bag, which he gives to BRUCE. BRUCE picks up his knife and tries to give it to SERGEANT COSTER, who refuses.*)

SERGEANT: I don't want your damn knife.

BRUCE: (*Looks down at PETER*) Is he dead?

SERGEANT: Nay, he just wishes he were.

BRUCE: What goin' happen to Pete?

SERGEANT: Don't worry about him. He'll be all right by the time he gets out on bail. (*Pauses.*) Say, how gooda friends are you guys? He's goin' need bail for assaulting a police officer, disturbing the peace, inciting rebellion, and threatenin' a Public Health official in the course of his duties. That outta be a few thousand. You wanna put up some bail money for your friend?

PETER: (*Moaning.*) What happened? Where am I?

(*Sirens are sounding in the background. SERGEANT COSTER pulls PETER to his feet.*)

SERGEANT: You're comin' with me buddy. You have the right to remain silent. Anything you say can and will be used against you in a court of law.

(*SERGEANT COSTER leads PETER off stage right. BRUCE and THOMAS look at one another. BRUCE looks down at THOMAS's name tag.*)

BRUCE: Dupont? Are you from out around Effie?

THOMAS: Yeah, my folks still live out there. What's your last name?

BRUCE: Maynard, Bruce Maynard's the name. (*Extends his free hand to THOMAS, who shakes it.*)

THOMAS: Are you Cecil and Clara's son?

BRUCE: The same.

THOMAS: Well I'll be damned. We're second cousins.

BRUCE: Ain't that something.

THOMAS: How do you cook them things, anyway?

BRUCE: You bake 'em in an oven at 375 degrees for about four hours. Every few minutes you cover 'em with them drippings. It's some kinda good. Serve it with yams and little onions in cream and you got you one heck of a Christmas coon. (*Presents the coon to THOMAS.*) Wanna keep it?

THOMAS: Nay. But thanks anyway. Besides, that's bribing a state official and I don't want any more trouble from you. . .cousin. (*Pauses.*) You need any help gettin' that box in your truck?

BRUCE: I'd be mighty obliged. . .cuz.

> (*BRUCE throws the coon into the box and slaps THOMAS on the back and the two of them pull the box off stage left. Lights out.*)

THE END

DAISY PATTERN PYSANKA

CAST OF CHARACTERS

CATHERINE: Middle aged woman, dressed in comfortable clothing, nothing particularly ethnic, but a skirt would be nice for the dancing sequence.

TATYANA: Middle aged woman, also dressed in comfortable clothing, perhaps a simple blouse and skirt.

SETTING

There is a table facing the audience with two chairs. On the table is pysanki making equipment: kistkas, wax, mason jars of colored dyes, candles, and eggs, both white and colored. There should be a basket of completed eggs if possible. Pysanki eggs are made by drawing on eggs with wax and then placing the eggs in progressively darker dyes. After completion, the wax is melted off and the eggs are varnished.

(*CATHERINE and TATYANA come on stage and light their candles. The lights go up to full. They begin heating their kistkas and drawing on the eggs during the play. Music for the entrance should be Kucmoch, a lively Czech folk tune.*)

CATHERINE: No! Never! She can die in Chicago. I never want to see or hear from her again.

TATYANA: That's not very charitable. I think you'll regret it. What if your mother dies before you get a chance to see her again?

CATHERINE: Too bad for her. (*Finishes an egg and holds it up to look at it.*) Pretty good, if I do say so myself.

TATYANA: (*Reaches over and takes the egg, which CATHERINE hands to her.*) Golly, you do beautiful work. Look at those lines. Straight as arrows. (*Hands the pysanka back to CATHERINE.*) You're really a pro.

I'll never get as good as you. (*Gets up to stretch.*) But I think you're wrong about your mother.

CATHERINE: (*Sets down her kistka.*) Why are you so interested in my mother anyway?

TATYANA: (*Wanders around looking at pysanki in the basket. Examines one of the eggs as she talks.*) My mother was a bitter woman too. She always felt my father was somehow not as good a catch as she deserved. She harangued my poor dad until the day he died. (*Turns around to face CATHERINE.*) I didn't know you could die from nagging. I guess my mother tried to prove it anyway.

CATHERINE: Your father died of colon cancer.

TATYANA: Yes, he did. But I'm sure the nagging didn't help.

CATHERINE: (*Holds up the egg she's working on.*) Look at the divisions of this pysanka. They form the sign of the cross. It's got a lot of white, green, and blue. No black at all. It's a cheerful pysanka.

TATYANA: Yes, it's beautiful and very happy looking. You send your pysanki all over the world? Why not send that one to your mother? I'm sure she'd love it.

CATHERINE: Stop babbling nonsense and get to work. You haven't even finished a dozen pysanki yet and there's only four weeks left until Easter. Leave my mother out of this.

TATYANA: (*Sits down and begins to work on an egg.*) I'm telling you, my mother was a bitter woman. She wanted everything just so. I had to wear skirts and those awful white stockings with dark shoes. We had to go to church for two hours on Sunday and again on Wednesday night. I couldn't play in the mud with the boys. I hated her as a child. But when my dad got really sick, she never left his side for a single minute.

43

CATHERINE: I thought you said she nagged your father to death. What did she do? Did she take care of him or did she nag him to death? You've got to make up your mind.

TATYANA: That's the odd part. She did both. (*Works on her pysanka.*) She told him he was killing her with all the extra work, but she changed his colostomy bag and wiped his butt like a little baby. I'd never seen anything like it. (*Examines her egg.*) Once I walked in on them when she was washing him. He was stark naked. Her hands went over his body with a tenderness I'd never seen before. I felt like a peeping Tom, a regular *voyeur.* (*Shakes her shoulders.*) It was almost like walking in on them while they were having sex. I did that once, too you know. (*Throws up her hands.*) Gosh! That almost cured me of having sex forever.

CATHERINE: Can you change the topic, please?

TATYANA: (*Examines her pysanka, and then shows it to CATHERINE.*) Do you think this part here ought to be green or yellow?

CATHERINE: Green.

TATYANA: (*Looks at the egg.*) Green, of course. The color of rebirth, renewal. (*Works on her pysanka.*) So what exactly did your mother do that was so unforgivable?

CATHERINE: (*Stands up and becomes animated, swinging her arms around.*) My mother weighed my father's meat! (*Imitates her mother's shrill voice.*) Here, Nicolas, here's your four ounces of ham. Not too much, now. And only two slices of bread, not four. We don't want you getting fat. (*Reverts to her usual speech pattern.*) Fat! My poor father was dying from lung cancer. And she denied him a few extra ounces of meat!

TATYANA: Maybe she was just frugal?

CATHERINE: Frugal? Heck no! She was evil. She rationed his meat, just like she rationed her love, a little tiny bit at a time. (*Imitates her mother's voice.*) Not too much, dear, you might get sick. (*Resumes her own voice.*) She was a wicked miser with her affections.

TATYANA: But you said your father was having an affair. Why didn't your mother just walk out on him? Before he got cancer?

CATHERINE: (*Swings around.*) That would've been too easy, too clean, too humane. No, she decided to stick around and weigh his meat. She weighed her words and her gestures. And all the while she watched Dad waste away from cancer, one pound at a time. She didn't even have the decency to tell me he was so sick. I had to learn from my in-laws. By the time I finally got to see him, he was as yellow as this dye. (*Points to a jar of yellow dye and looks like she is going to cry.*) He looked like a yellow skeleton. I'll never forgive her. No! Never! She can rot up there in Chicago.

(*TATYANA stands up and comes over to comfort CATHERINE. CATHERINE pulls away. They stop and look at each other.*)

TATYANA: Don't get mad at me. I'm just here making pysanki. (*Goes over to CATHERINE.*) This is a good time for a little break. Show me the steps to that new dance. I haven't quite gotten it yet. I don't want to mess up like in last year's performance.

CATHERINE: (*Shakes her head.*) I'm really not in a dancing mood.

TATYANA: Come on. We're supposed to be in a good psychological place to make pysanki. Remember, no gossip, not bad thoughts, no hatred. You told me that yourself.

CATHERINE: (*Sighs.*) Yes. That's the theory. Each egg is supposed to be a symbolic gift, a blessed talisman, pure in thought and design. I told you that too.

TATYANA: Yes. You did. Now show me the steps to that new lady's dance.

(CATHERINE goes to a little CD player and puts on the music to the dance "Doulanske Louky," taught be Vonnie Brown. It's a slow woman's dance. CATHERINE takes TATYANA's hand.)

CATHERINE: Now follow me. Right, then right, then right, then forward, then back, and then pause. Good. Again. *(They dance.)* Now comes the fast part. *(The women dance as a couple. CATHERINE goes over and turns off the music.)* That was fine. Now let's get back to work.

TATYANA: Thanks. I think I got it. *(Looks over at CATHERINE's pysanka.)* That's a beautiful egg. I like the daisy pattern.

CATHERINE: We had daisies at our house in Chicago. There was a miniscule back yard and my mother worked like a dog back there. There was hardly any sun and just a little bit of nasty mud. But somehow she got those darn daisies to grow. *(Looks at the egg.)* She would cut a few each day during the spring and summer and put them in a vase on the table. It was so pitiful, but it was also somehow sweet, even tender.

TATYANA: And when your father died, did she give him some daisies?

CATHERINE: *(Looks up.)* How'd you know that?

TATYANA: Just a lucky guess.

CATHERINE: Yes. Yes, she did. She put some daisies in his hands, right there in the coffin. It was like some token of love that she never managed to give him when he was alive. *(Pauses.)* I'll never forget those daisies. When I saw them, I hated her and loved her at the same time. It's the first time I cried after his death.

TATYANA: I bet she would love it.

CATHERINE: Love what?

TATYANA: Your daisy pysanka. It doesn't have any black. No colors of death. Just green, and yellow, and white, and blue. It's a beautiful egg. It's a real expression of love. Perhaps from someone who might not know how to express it any other way? (*Pauses and looks at her CATHERINE.*) Send it to your mother for Easter.

CATHERINE: (*Reaches over and grabs TATYANA's hand and squeezes it.*) I just can't do it. Not yet.

TATYANA: Of course you can. If not now, when? This pysanka is beautiful. You're beautiful. Do it now, not when your mother's dead.

CATHERINE: (*Pulls away from TATYANA and glares at her.*) My mother is already dead to me.

TATYANA: No, she's not dead. Burying her in your mind makes you as uncharitable as she was. You're just like her, only younger.

CATHERINE: Don't you dare compare me with that hateful woman! (*Trembling with rage, she raises her hand to strike TATYANA.*)

TATYANA: (*Does not budge.*) Why not? You're rationing your eggs like she rationed your father's meat. What's the difference? Give her something beautiful now while she's alive. Not when she's gone. You know I'm right.

> (*TATYANA puts her arms around CATHERINE, who cries a little. At first CATHERINE does not react. But she ends by hugging her friend.*)

TATYANA: Why waste of a work of art by putting it in a casket? That would be a real tragedy.

CATHERINE: (*Pulls away from TATYANA and laughs a little.*) They did that, you know? They used to put pysanki in caskets as good luck charms for the dead. Something to help them on their way to heaven.

(*Takes the daisy pysanka and holds it up.*) I hate to admit it, but you're right. And I don't want to be like my mother.

TATYANA: Then don't be. It's a choice. Bury your hatred, not this egg. (*Takes the egg from CATHERINE and examines it, turning it around in her hand.*) This pysanka is too lovely to bury.

CATHERINE: (*Takes the egg back from TATYANA and gently sets it on the table.*) I'll do it. I'll send it to her.

TATYANA: Promise?

CATHERINE: I promise.

TATYANA: Good for you! So that's decided. (*Pulls CATHERINE away from the table.*) Now come and let's stretch our legs with a little dance practice. Remember, we need to be in a good spiritual mood for any more pysanki making. (*Blows out the candles.*)

(*CATHERINE gets up and the two women dance off the stage to the haunting tune of "Louky." Lights dim to dark.*)

THE END

EL KAFIR AND HUNT

CAST OF CHARACTERS

MOHAMED EL KAFIR: Naturalized American accused of supporting terrorism. He speaks with a mild Middle Eastern accent.

CHARLES HUNT: Court-appointed defense attorney.

SETTING

There is a table and two chairs in an otherwise bare room. The silhouette of a barred window projects on the ground, giving the impression of a prison room.

EL KAFIR: And what if I don't want a defense attorney?

HUNT: That would be an error, Mr. Kafir.

EL KAFIR: It's Mohamed, Mohamed El Kafir.

HUNT: How exactly would you like me to address you?

EL KAFIR: Mohamed or Mamoud, if you prefer. That's what my family calls me. Why not be on a first name basis? May I call you Charles or do you prefer Chuck?

HUNT: I prefer Mr. Hunt. But if you insist, Charles is fine.

EL KAFIR: Charles, I don't believe in your system of justice. So why should I not organize my own defense?

HUNT: Because you lack any knowledge of the mechanisms and vocabulary of our legal system.

EL KAFIR: Ah yes, your legal system. That's the one where everyone sues everyone and lawyers get a half of everything the client wins.

HUNT: That's in civil cases, not criminal ones.

EL KAFIR: Taking a third or even a half of the client's award seems pretty criminal to me. In fact, it sounds like highway robbery. Plus it has to encourage frivolous litigation. Isn't that what you people do, sue each other all the time for everything?

HUNT: Mr. El Kafir, Mohamed, our legal system is not on trial here, you are. And I don't get anything more than the court allowed fees for my services. And that's not a lot.

EL KAFIR: Of course.

HUNT: Can we get back to business here, please?

EL KAFIR: Of course.

HUNT: (*Takes a pad and pen.*) Now, let's cut to the chase.

EL KAFIR: The chase, of course.

HUNT: Did you conspire to collect funds to send to a terrorist organization?

EL KAFIR: That depends.

HUNT: On what?

EL KAFIR: On your definition of terrorism.

HUNT: Let me rephrase the question. Did you collect money for the Palestinian Children's Education and Welfare Fund?

EL KAFIR: Yes. We had a jar on the counter and we collected funds for that organization.

HUNT: Did you know that the Palestinian Children's Fund was sending money to Al-Qaeda?

EL KAFIR: No.

HUNT: You did NOT know that the money from that fund went to Al-Qaeda?

EL KAFIR: No. I did not know, but I suspected it.

HUNT: How so?

EL KAFIR: Because the gentleman who came by to collect the money from us said that it may be used in any way and anywhere the organization felt was in the best interest of the children of Palestine.

HUNT: Do you want to go to jail?

EL KAFIR: Do Palestinian children in Gaza want to stay in their country, which happens to be a prison? Does anyone want to suffer injustice at the hands of the Jewish-Fascist state?

HUNT: I don't think such comments will be helpful to you or your defense, especially in court.

EL KAFIR: May I stand up?

HUNT: Of course.

EL KAFIR: (*Stands and begins to walk around.*) Do you have any children, Charles?

HUNT: I really don't see how this is going to help in your defense, but yes, I have three.

EL KAFIR: So do I. What are their names?

HUNT: I don't think you need that information and I'm not interested in letting you have it.

EL KAFIR: So you're afraid of me, too?

HUNT: I'm your court-appointed defense attorney, not your friend.

EL KAFIR: Of course. (*Pauses.*) I also have three children, as I mentioned. There names are Yusef, Fatima and Momed.

HUNT: Please, Mr. El Kafir, we don't have much time together. Is this information really necessary?

EL KAFIR: Yes. I have three children, Yusef, who's eleven, Fatima, who's eight, and Momed, who's three. (*Turns to CHARLES.*) I love my children and they love me, such as children can. They don't want to lose their father, especially for something trivial. (*Pauses.*) But this is not trivial. I live in this country. I appreciate the fact that I can live and work in peace. (*Raises his voice.*) But I do not appreciate the war-mongering. I do not appreciate the children of my brothers and sisters being bombed and brutalized. I cannot sleep thinking of my fellow Muslims dying for their faith while I live peacefully in this land.

HUNT: But you do live in this land. And you still must abide by the laws of the land. And those laws prohibit the funding of organizations which seek the destruction of the very country you live in.

EL KAFIR: There are moral dictates which require civil disobedience. Did not your own Henry David Thoreau say that? Did not Martin Luther King? Did not your prophet, Jesus?

HUNT: For heaven's sake, I need to convince twelve of your fellow citizens that you did not know that fund went to Al-Qaeda and that you don't need to go to prison for life.

EL KAFIR: For heaven's sake is why I do it. And I am sure that even if I should die, I will stand before Allah and receive his blessing and join with those who have gone before me in martyrdom for the faith. (*Pauses.*) Charles, are you a religious man?

HUNT: This is not relevant here. Please, let's get back to business.

EL KAFIR: But that is the business. Faith is the business at hand. And I have faith in the justice of our cause and I have no faith in your system of justice. It's a simple as that. Are you a religious man?

HUNT: I'm spiritual without being formally religious.

EL KAFIR: So you do not believe in a life after death?

HUNT: Please, can we get back to the question at hand?

EL KAFIR: Your faith is the question at hand, Charles. If I give you the opportunity, will you accept Allah as your only God and Mohamed as his prophet?

HUNT: (*Shakes his head.*) I believe we're finished here.

EL KAFIR: So you are an infidel? You are not even a believer in the book?

HUNT: What are you talking about?

EL KAFIR: The book, the Koran, the Torah, the Old Testament. Mohamed said we can spare those who believe in the book, that means Jews or Christians. But the others are infidels and may be killed with his blessing.

HUNT: That's enough. We're done here. Guard!

EL KAFIR: Not quite.

HUNT: What do you mean? Not quite? Guard!

EL KAFIR: (*Plunges toward CHARLES and grabs him by the throat.*) I must kill you with my hands and my salvation will be assured.

HUNT: (*Tries to get away, but MOHAMED grabs him and pushes him to the ground.*) Help! Guards! Help!

EL KAFIR: Die! Die, you faithless pig!

HUNT: Help! Help!

(*CHARLES struggles and manages to push off MOHAMED, who falls backward. CHARLES rushes toward the door, but finds that it's locked. CHARLES pounds with his fists, but no one seems to hear.*)

HUNT: Guards! Help!

(*MOHAMED Gets up and rushes to CHARLES and tackles him. They fall on the floor and MOHAMED finishes strangling CHARLES, who goes limp. Then MOHAMED gets up and brushes off his hands and sits back at the table.*)

EL KAFIR: Okay. That was pretty good. Now get up and let's try it again with reversed roles.

HUNT: (*Gets up and brushes himself off.*) That was darn good, if I do say so myself. (*Looks around.*) Okay, now I'm Mohamed this time. Ready?

EL KAFIR: Ready.

HUNT: (*Yells in a Middle Easter accent.*) And what if I don't want a defense attorney?

(*Lights dim to dark.*)

THE END

FIBROMANIACAL

CAST OF CHARACTERS

DR. ALFRED TURNLEY: He is a middle aged to older doctor, dressed in a white coat. He is distinguished looking and should wear a tie, which adds to his aura of dignity and authority.

BETTY-LOU PRITCHARD: She is a young to middle aged woman, dressed in causal and clean clothing. She has an abrasive personality and manner.

DORIS TURNLEY: Devoted wife of Dr. Turnley. She is also very dignified, with a hint of the unconventional. She exudes sweetness and light. She is mildly stooped and wears a tightly bound head scarf.

SETTING

A doctor's office. There is a desk with a lamp and some papers. Dr. Turnley is seated in a chair and there are two chairs in front of the desk for visitors.

(*DR. TURNLEY is seated at the desk and is going through papers. He signs some and places them on one pile. The others he does not sign and puts them in another pile. MRS. BETTY-LOU PRITCHARD comes in. She is belligerent and agitated.*)

BETTY: Are you Dr. Alfred Turnley?

ALFRED: Yes I am. How can I help you today?

(*ALFRED rises to greet her and extends his hand to shake hers. BETTY-LOU refuses and ALFRED sits back down. ALFRED indicates one of the visitor's chairs.*)

BETTY: No! I don't want to sink to your level.

ALFRED: Do you mind telling me what this is all about Mrs. . . . ?

BETTY: Pritchard, Mrs. Betty-Lou Pritchard. (*Shoves a paper in his face as she speaks.*) Is that your name and your signature at the bottom of this paper?

ALFRED: Yes. That is my name and signature.

BETTY: Do you recognize the document?

ALFRED: Yes. It's a denial of services. I have to review all requests on behalf of the insurance company.

BETTY: Yes, a denial of services for important mitochondrial ATP diagnostic tests, a denial for the use of the medications *Lyrica, Savella* and *Cymbalta* together, and a denial for trans-cutaneous electro-stimulation. Are you the one who denied all of these things?

ALFRED: Yes. I did.

BETTY: Aren't you aware that these are legitimate tests and recognized medications for the treatment of fibromyalgia?

ALFRED: Yes. They are recognized if you happen to believe in that particular disease. In your case, however, I was not convinced of a diagnosis of fibromyalgia.

BETTY: (*Looks wounded.*) In my case? In my case! I have been diagnosed by one of the world-renowned experts in fibromyalgia. (*Spins around and points all over her body.*) I have eleven out of eighteen painful trigger points and I also have chronic fatigue, and depression, and irritable bowel syndrome. I have suffered for years, not just months. And although this may not be something you happen to believe in, fibromyalgia is a debilitating disease recognized by the American

College of Rheumatology. What retrograde planet do you happen to come from, Dr. Troglodyte Turnley?

ALFRED: With all due respect, the diagnosis remains unsubstantiated in many, if not all, cases. And there is still considerable difference of opinion about the disease among respectable medical specialists. In addition, there is almost always an unmistakable supra-tentorial component in most patients.

BETTY: Supra what?

ALFRED: Supra-tentorial.

BETTY: What does that mean?

ALFRED: It means above the tentorium of the brain in the cerebral cortex. In other words, psychological.

BETTY: (*Screams.*) You're a quack! A quack and an insurance company whore! I'll sue you and take this whole office from your undeserving hands. I may be sick and tired and depressed, but I am fired up with the sacred fire of justice. I will do it, if not for me, than for all the other suffering women out there who are also being denied life-restoring treatments. (*Pauses.*) Mark my words, Dr. Turkey.

ALFRED: Turnley.

BETTY: TURKEY! You will not have this high paid cushy job denying insurance claims much longer. You will be drawing blood in a lab somewhere, if they'll have you. As God is my witness, you are going down and your miserable insurance company is going down with you.

> (*DORIS TURNLEY comes in. DORIS is a distinguished woman, wearing a handkerchief as a scarf over her head. DORIS carries a tray with a teapot and a couple of mugs and walks haltingly, as if in pain.*)

DORIS: Alfred, your tea is ready. Is this a bad time to come in?

ALFRED: Of course not.

BETTY: Oh my God. Your receptionist brings in hot tea. What do you have to pay this poor old lady to do this kind of menial labor? And in that get-up no less. Maybe you've got her fooled, but your sure can't fool me.

ALFRED: Mrs. Pritchard, this is my wife, Doris.

(*BETTY-LOU looks surprised. DORIS smiles and bows her head.*)

DORIS: So nice to meet you Mrs. Pritchard.

BETTY: You're his wife?

DORIS: Yes, for the last forty years and I wouldn't change a single day for all the gold in the world. I'm such a blessed woman to have such a good husband. (*She indicates the tray.*) Would you like a cup of tea? It's a special herbal blend.

BETTY: No. No thank you.

(*A silence follows. ALFRED sips his tea. DORIS does not touch her cup.*)

BETTY: (*To DORIS*) I don't know if you're aware of what your husband does, Mrs. Turnley, but he is denying care to people like me that suffer from fibromyalgia, a very debilitating physical disorder.

ALFRED: I don't discuss medical cases with my wife. That's a violation of your privacy and a very serious offense. Besides, I'm sure my wife is not interested in the specifics of any individual cases.

DORIS: I would never dream of interfering with my husband's work, but I'm always interested in people and their medical problems as long as they are willing to share their story. You say you suffer from fibromyalgia?

BETTY: Yes. I am one of the worst cases that Dr. Horton, a world-renowned specialist in Dallas, has ever seen. He said that I would be functionally crippled within a matter of years or even months without intensive electro-stimulation and multiple drug therapy. And your husband is denying me much needed tests and life saving treatments just to save the insurance company some money.

DORIS: Dr. George Frederick Horton?

BETTY: Yes. He's famous around the United States and around the world. Do you know him?

DORIS: Oh, heavens yes. He is my brother's second cousin, and one of the most notorious crooks in the medical professions. (*Laughs.*)

BETTY: That's a lie!

DORIS: Oh no, it's not. He is going to be indicted for Medicare and Medicaid fraud in the very near future, if he hasn't been already. They say he soaked Medicare for millions of dollars for questionable treatments as well as off-label drug use. Not only that, but he was getting money directly from the pharmaceutical companies under the table at the same time. Kick backs, I believe they're called. Why it's a crying shame. He was such a promising young man, smart and good-looking, too.

BETTY: I don't believe you.

DORIS: You can believe me or not. (*Indicates her untouched cup.*) Are you sure you don't want some herbal tea. I haven't touched mine yet. Please try some. It's a special medicinal preparation by the great Hindu healer, Rajmahanderwal. He really is world famous, and justifiably so.

BETTY: (*Looks skeptical, but takes the cup and sips.*) This is good. Really good.

DORIS: Yes, it tastes good, but how do you feel?

BETTY: I feel better. I really feel much better. It's incredible.

DORIS: How about your pain, your fatigue, your depression, and all that stiffness in your trigger points?

(*DORIS goes over and leads BETTY-LOU to a chair. Then DORIS begins massaging BETTY's shoulders.*)

BETTY: Wow! That feels so good. (*Takes another big gulp of the tea.*)

DORIS: Feel the healing powers of the liquid going into your body. Taste the restorative herbs. Let all that pain and tension drift away as your dark mood lifts.

BETTY: That feels wonderful. It's like a miracle.

ALFRED: Honey, how about me? I've got quite a bit of tension, too. (*Points to his shoulders and neck.*) Here and here and here. I have all those trigger points.

(*DORIS goes over and massages ALFRED.*)

DORIS: Relax. Let my hands knead away the knots. Feel my healing fingers massaging away the tension.

ALFRED: I feel so much better. (*Pats DORIS on the hand.*) Thank you, honey. I love you so much.

DORIS: I love you too. If you want any more tea, please let me know. (*To BETTY-LOU*) How about you, dear, any more tea?

BETTY: (*Extends her cup*). I'd love some.

(*DORIS pours the tea, then gathers up the tray and teapot and walks off stage with some difficulty.*)

BETTY: She's so sweet.

ALFRED: Yes. She's a great person, a great wife. (*Wipes away a tear.*)

BETTY: What's wrong?

ALFRED: No, it's nothing. It's not your problem. I'd rather not discuss it.

BETTY: No, really. I want to know. I love to see older couples that adore one another after so many years. All I got was an abusive dickhead for a husband and he walked out on me years ago.

ALFRED: I'm so sorry for you. Everyone deserves the blessings of a long and happy marriage. When I look at my wife, I think of that poem, "Come grow old with me, the best is yet to be, the last of life for which the first was made is now at hand." (*Pauses.*) If only we could.

BETTY: Why can't you?

AFRED: She's got metastatic breast cancer and there's nothing left to do now that's she's finished chemotherapy. She's dying a slow, painful death.

BETTY: I'm so sorry.

ALFRED: I'm sorry, too. (*Pauses.*) About your request, you can fill out an appeal and I assure you that the insurance company will reconsider. They will give it to another physician who might by more sympathetic to your circumstances.

BETTY: (*Tears up the document.*) Forget it. I'm feeling a lot better now. Maybe you're right. Maybe it's all just in my head. (*Begins to leave, and then turns back.*) By the way, could you have your wife send me the name of that Indian guy who makes the healing tea?

ALFRED: Of course. Good luck to you.

(*BETTY-LOU leaves stage left. DORIS re-enters on stage right and is carrying a tray with some cookies.*)

DORIS: I thought you both might like some home-made chocolate chip cookies.

ALFRED: Home-made my ass. These are from McDonalds. You haven't made a cookie in twenty years. (*Takes a bite.*) Would you take off that handkerchief, you look like a babushka.

(*DORIS slips off the handkerchief, revealing a full head of hair.*)

ALFRED: You are so good. We just saved the insurance company $50,000 in useless treatments. That means another $1000 bonus for us. At this rate, we'll have that condo in Colorado paid for in no time.

DORIS: Did you give me metastatic breast cancer or Lou Gehrig's Disease this time?

ALFRED: Metastatic breast cancer. It works every time.

(*They laugh and eat cookies. Lights out.*)

THE END

GRAND ILLUSIONS: PROSPERITY, INSIGHT AND SIBLING LOVE

(A One Act Family Drama

in Three Scenes)

CAST OF CHARACTERS

LORI WOODHILL: Dan and Helen's daughter. She is Fred's mother and Brian's wife.

BRIAN WOODHILL: Lori's husband. He is middle aged and Fred's father.

FRED WOODHILL: Lori and Brian's son (an older teenager).

EMMA: Fred's girlfriend.

FRANK HUNTER: Dan and Helen's son. He is middle-aged. He is Steve's father and Lori's brother.

SUSAN HUNTER: Frank's wife. She is also middle-aged. She is Steve's mother.

STEVE HUNTER: Frank and Susan's young adult son.

DAN HUNTER: Elderly man and father to Lori and Frank.

HELEN HUNTER: Dan's wife and mother to Lori and Frank.

SETTINGS

Vary according to the scenes.

AUTHORS NOTE

Each scene is one of family illusions of one sort or another. Scene I requires four actors, Scene II requires three and Scene III, three. The scenes may be played together (requiring nine actors) or played separately.

SCENE I (ILLUSION ONE: PROSPERITY)

CHARACTERS

LORI: Middle-aged woman, a bit frumpy.

BRIAN: Lori's husband. Also middle-aged. He may be a bit overweight.

FRED: Son of Lori and Brian. He is seventeen or eighteen years old. He is dressed in black, with a silver chain attached to his wallet. His hair is short, but not shaved.

EMMA: Steve's girlfriend. She is assured and articulate. Neither she nor Steve looks punk, but they do reflect current tastes in clothing. She wears no makeup and might have short, unnaturally black hair in a pageboy cut. She wears a loose-fitting wrinkled shirt over faded blue jeans with frayed cuffs and Birkenstock sandals.

SETTING

There is a dinner table on stage left that Lori is setting. Stage right has a couch and chairs as well as a low coffee table. There is a piece of furniture that serves as a bar.

(LORI *spreads a faux Provençal tablecloth on the dining room table. She distributes matching red placements and a set of the square dishes from Pottery Barn. She frames each plate with appropriate silverware and adds the water and wine glasses. There is a centerpiece, a fall themed floral arrangement, which complements the red and yellow color scheme. Intense California sun shines through French doors to the patio and illuminates the table. She steps back to admire the effect. She hears the front door open and shut.*)

BRIAN: Lori, I'm home. (*BRIAN enters stage right.*)

LORI: I'm here! In the dining room! Come see.

BRIAN: (*Peeks into the dining room and examines the table.*) Very nice. I need a drink.

LORI: Sure.

(*LORI goes to a bar pours two scotch and waters. BRIAN sits on the couch in the living room. BRIAN starts to prop his heels onto the coffee table, but stops and sets them back on the floor.*)

LORI: So how was your day?

BRIAN: Where did all that new stuff come from on the dining room table?

LORI: What stuff?

BRIAN: The dishes, the tablecloth, the candlesticks, the flowers.

LORI: Don't be upset. It was all on sale. Fifty percent off at Pottery Barn. I couldn't resist.

(*BRIAN takes a huge gulp from his glass and LORI does the same.*)

BRIAN: Do you know how much I made today?

LORI: No.

BRIAN: Two hundred dollars, maybe not even that.

LORI: It didn't cost that much, I swear.

BRIAN: Lori, we're broke. I'm not making any money. We can't pay the mortgage. And you're buying a bunch of crap from Pottery Barn. For heaven's sake, what are you thinking?

LORI: It's Fred's birthday, his eighteenth birthday. He's inviting his girlfriend over. Can we at least make a nice impression?

BRIAN: Which girl friend?

LORI: Emma. She's very pretty and extraverted, a nice girl, and Fred really likes her.

BRIAN: He's eighteen. He's going to have a bunch of girl friends in college. Speaking of college, did he make up his mind about which one he's going to?

LORI: He'd like to go to Columbia.

BRIAN: He can't go to Columbia.

LORI: Why?

BRIAN: Because they only offer partial scholarships.

LORI: Maybe we can. . . .

BRIAN: What? Not eat? Borrow more money? With what collateral? We already owe more on this house than it's worth. (*Finishes off his glass with one gulp.*) He has to stay in state, the closer the better. He doesn't have a choice. (*Pauses.*) We don't have a choice.

LORI: And if I got a job?

BRIAN: What job?

LORI: Any job. I saw they were looking for cashiers at the Super One.

BRIAN: And who's going to drive Fred to debate team after school, and tutoring, and whatever else he does?

LORI: He could drive himself.

BRIAN: How? We can't afford insurance for him. It's over $500 dollars for six months. We're broke and you're buying dishes to impress his girlfriend. I need another drink.

(*LORI takes his glass and stands up. She goes to the bar and pours another rink. She takes a plate of cheese squares and crackers. The front door bell rings. LORI delivers the drink and food to BRIAN, who sits motionless on the couch. She goes to the front door and opens it. EMMA stands in the doorway, with FRED at her side.*)

EMMA: Hi, Mrs. Woodhill. I drove Fred home from school in my car. I thought it would save you a trip.

LORI: Hello Emma. Thank you so much. Come in, please.

(*FRED and EMMA go in and sit on two chairs facing the couch.*)

EMMA: Hello, Mr. Woodhill.

BRIAN: Hello Emma, Fred. How was your day?

EMMA: Great! I just got accepted to Columbia.

LORI: That's wonderful for you. (*Glances from FRED to BRIAN as she speaks.*) Something to drink? A coke? Orange juice?

EMMA: Orange juice, please, as long as it's organic.

LORI: (*Hesitates.*) I'm not really sure about that.

EMMA: I always use organic. Everything's so full of pesticides these days.

BRIAN: Columbia, eh? That's terrific. Fred would like to go there, too, but I think he's probably going to have to stay closer to home, at a state school.

EMMA: That's too bad. It would be so cool if we could both go to Columbia. (*Turns to FRED and puts her hand on his knee.*) Wouldn't it?

FRED: (*Answers in an emotionless monotone.*) Yeah, that would be cool.

> (*LORI goes to the bar and hurries back with two glasses of orange juice. LORI hands them to the EMMA and FRED.*)

LORI: I think it's organic. (*Turns to BRIAN.*) Another scotch?

BRIAN: (*Shoves his glass in her directions.*) That would be great, thanks honey.

> (*LORI returns to the bar and pours two more generous scotch and waters and returns to the group.*)

EMMA: My parents always wanted me to go to Rhodes, but that seemed so pretentious to me. And I couldn't bear to go anyplace that's not a thousand miles from California. So Columbia seemed like a great choice.

LORI: It's a bit pricey, isn't it?

EMMA: Oh no! It's only $46,000 tuition, plus room and board, of course, and travel. For such a prestigious school, that's a real bargain. At least that's what my parents say.

FRED: I couldn't go there even if I were accepted.

LORI: Oh, I don't know. It might be a stretch, but we could possibly manage.

(*LORI looks over at BRIAN for some support, but he continues to stare into his glass.*)

FRED: We can't afford it. Why bother talking about it?

(*A long silence follows.*)

LORI: I hope you like chicken?

EMMA: (*Shakes her head.*) I don't eat animal protein, Mrs. Woodhill. Well, nothing with eyes and a mother.

BRIAN: (*Laughs out loud.*) That's a lot of things. No eyes and a mother.

LORI: Chickens have eyes.

BRIAN: And mothers.

EMMA: No chicken for me. I went vegan last year. I tied to convince Fred, but he's so stubborn. He said he didn't want to put any additional cooking burdens on his mother. (*Looks at LORI.*) That's so sweet, isn't it?

LORI: We were supposed to have shrimp cocktail.

EMMA: Nope. Eyes and mothers.

LORI: And chocolate mousse?

EMMA: Afraid not. It's made with animal protein. Besides, most cacao beans are harvested by miserable peasants under exploitative conditions. You really have to be so careful. Food's not just nourishment, it's a political statement of social solidarity, isn't it, Freddie?

(*FRED nods. Both LORI and BRIAN tale large gulps of their drinks.*)

LORI: We have a salad, would that be all right? With croutons and bits of cheese?

EMMA: (*Shakes her head.*) Animal proteins. I'd have to pick out all the cheese. That would be so hard.

> (*BRIAN stands up and takes out his wallet. He extracts forty dollars and hands them to FRED.*)

BRIAN: This is for you, son. Go have a nice dinner at that vegan place downtown. Happy birthday.

> (*FRED and EMMA stand up simultaneously. Neither has touched their orange juice. FRED reaches forward, leaning over the coffee table, and takes the money from his father.*)

FRED: Are you sure? I know how tight money is around here.

BRIAN: Yes, I'm sure. Happy birthday.

FRED: Thanks Dad. (*Pockets the money. Steps around the coffee table and hugs BRIAN before turning to LORI.*) Are you sure? I know you went to a lot of trouble to prepare the dinner.

LORI: Of course, dear.

> (*FRED and EMMA leave. LORI returns to the couch and sits down next to BRIAN.*)

LORI: I'm so sorry.

BRIAN: Bitch!

LORI: Me!

BRIAN: No, Emma, of course. I'm so glad she'll be at Columbia and he'll be right here in state. Out of sight, out of mind. (*Stands up and reaches to LORI and takes her by the hands.*) Let's eat. The table looks beautiful. The menu sound's great. And I couldn't ask for better company.

LORI: Really?

(*BRIAN takes LORI into his arms and gives her a warm hug.*)

BRIAN: Really!

(*BRIAN leads LORI to the dining room table. BRIAN pulls out a chair and invites LORI to sit down. Lights dim to dark.*)

SCENE II (ILLUSION 2: INSIGHT)

CHARACTERS

FRANK: A heavy-set middle aged man. He is casually dressed. He speaks in a self-assured way.

SUSAN: Frank's wife. She is also middle-aged, well dressed and speaks correctly.

STEVE: Frank and Susan's adult son. He is casually dressed, perhaps in a shirt and jeans. He wears a baseball cap, which makes him appear younger than he is.

SETTING

Frank and Susan are sitting at a kitchen table. He is leafing through documents. She is looking at a book of recipes. There is a bowl of green beans on the table as well.

SUSAN: This recipe looks good. Marinated beef tips with fresh asparagus and hollandaise sauce.

FRANK: It makes me sick!

SUSAN: Hollandaise?

FRANK: No, of course not. (*Shoves a paper over to SUSAN.*) Look at this!

SUSAN: What is it?

FRANK: It's dad's bank statement.

SUSAN: So.

FRANK: Look at this. (*Points to the paper.*) It's a $1,200 monthly withdrawal.

SUSAN: So, what is it?

FRANK: It's a mortgage payment.

SUSAN: Your parents have owned their own home for 50 years. A mortgage on what?

FRANK: My sister and brother-in-law's home, of course. It makes me physically ill. This has been going on for three years.

SUSAN: How do you even know about this?

FRANK: Because as prospective power of attorney and future executor of their estate, I get doubles of their financial statement. Supposedly it's to familiarize me with their accounts.

SUSAN: So what does it matter if Mom and Dad pay the mortgage? They can afford it.

(*FRANK stands up and replaces the statement in a binder.*)

FRANK: It's the principle. My folks are just enabling! They are keeping Lori and Brian in a perpetual state of infantilism. It's an outrage! Mom and Dad just won't set limits. Dad won't do the tough love thing. It's a disgrace!

(*SUSAN sets down the cookbook and reaches for the bowl of green beans. SUSAN pushes it in FRANK's direction.*)

SUSAN: Here. Help me break off the ends of the green beans.

(*FRANK sits down and takes a bean. FRANK snaps off one end and then the other with an aggressive determination unrelated to the bean.*)

SUSAN: And what about our own son, Steven?

FRANK: What about him?

SUSAN: We take care of Patricia four times a week.

FRANK: But she's our granddaughter. That's completely different.

SUSAN: Yes, and Lori and Brian are Dad and Mom's daughter and son-in-law. They're just trying to help them out of a tough economic situation.

FRANK: No, it's not the same. Patricia is a little girl, not a grown woman.

SUSAN: And Steven is a grown man, even if he is still our son.

FRANK: No! Steven is working hard and has struggled as a single father. He has weird shifts and there just isn't any way he can take care of Patricia without our help. Lori and Brian are both able-bodied adults and should both be working. Their kids are old enough to take care of themselves and they are just frittering away their time. They've just made a series of bad decisions and they're still making them.

SUSAN: Like Steve? Like having a child in his teens and not maintaining a single stable relationship for decades?

FRANK: I still don't think the situations are comparable.

(*The doorbell interrupts their conversation. SUSAN gets up and lets STEVE in through the kitchen door. He is dressed in his working cloths, including a baseball cap. He kisses SUSAN's cheek.*)

STEVE: Hi Mom. Hi Dad.

SUSAN: Maybe you want to help us get these green beans ready?

STEVE: Naw, no manual labor for me after work. (*Pulls up a chair and sits at the table.*)

FRANK: What's up?

STEVE: They've changed my shift at work again. Would you mind picking up Patty at school and keeping her tonight again?

FRANK: Of course not.

(*FRANK looks over at SUSAN, who gives him an inquisitive look.*)

STEVE: And she might have some homework, too. She has a social studies project or something like that.

FRANK: Any specific subject?

STEVE: Something to do about a state. I think she picked Louisiana. (*Pauses and picks up a green bean, which he twirls around his fingers before plopping back in the bowl.*) She only told me yesterday. She's got to get a bunch of pictures about the state, state bird, state flower, state song, and some famous people from there. And she needs to get one of those special display boards, you know, the ones that fold out in three. (*Picks up another two beans as if to demonstrate the board.*)

SUSAN: And when is this due?

STEVE: Tomorrow, of course. (*Pops one of the beans in his mouth. He mashes on it a moment before spitting it out in his hand and depositing it onto the table.*) Yeah, I know. It's short notice. But my printer's broken and then they changed the shifts on me. And Patty didn't tell me about the project until this morning, of course. She can be such a real devil some time.

SUSAN: Anything else?

STEVE: Well, it's getting close to Halloween and Patty said she wanted to be a princess. I mean like a real one, with a big gown and a crown and all that. I know you're a terrific seamstress. (*Grabs SUSAN's hand.*) Could you make her a princess costume. Oh pretty please.

SUSAN: I'm involved with a big project with the historical society right now. (*Extracts her hands from his.*)

STEVE: I know you can do it, Mom. You're so organized you can do ten things at once. Can you do it, just this one time?

SUSAN: (*Turns to FRANK and smiles.*) What to you think, dear? Do you think we can help Steve out by keeping Patricia, and doing the social studies project and making a Halloween costume?

(*FRANK does not answer. FRANK snaps the end off another bean.*)

SUSAN: Or would we just be enabling?

STEVE: Enabling, what does that mean?

SUSAN: Your father might know. Don't you, dear?

FRANK: (*Looks at STEVE's expectant face. After a long pause, FRANK answers.*) It's complicated.

STEVE: (*Shrugs his shoulders and looks away.*) I don't have time for any long explanations anyway. Maybe another time. (*Turns back to his mother.*) So you'll pick Patty up at school?

SUSAN: Of course, dear.

STEVE: And you'll help her do the social studies project?

SUSAN: Of course, dear.

STEVE: And you'll work on a princess costume for Halloween?

SUSAN: Of course, dear.

FRANK: I hope you'll at least pitch in and buy the school supplies and the sewing materials, won't you?

STEVE: Dad, you know how much they pay me. I can't afford things like that. (*Stands up and replaces his baseball cap as he heads for the back door.*) I'd really like to help, but I had some unexpected bills with my new girlfriend. You know what I mean. (*Flashes a big smile and winks at FRANK as he does out the door.*)

(*FRANK picks up another bean and pinches of the end with the aggressive gesture of a decapitation.*)

SUSAN: (*Imitates FRANK's voice.*) Dad just won't set any limits, eh? No tough love, eh? A disgrace, eh? (*Reaches into the bowl and picks out a few more beans, which SUSAN plops down in front of FRANK. Resumes her normal voice.*) Some more green beans, dear?

FRANK: Sure, why not? (*Grabs a bean and holds it close to his face as he snaps off the end. Lights dim to dark.*)

SCENE III (ILLUSION 3: SIBLING LOVE)

CHARACTERS:

DAN: An elderly man with obvious mobility issues. He is casually dressed.

HELEN: Dan's wife. She is just as old and is also casually dressed.

LORI: Dan and Helen's middle aged daughter. She is also casually dressed.

SETTING

There is a large table stage right. About mid-stage, there is some sort of low wall, which separates the stage into two parts. It actually separates the "formal dining room" from the "den."

(*DAN wipes the sweat off his forehead and brushes back his hair before grabbing a card table and pulling it into the "den" from stage left. DAN sets it down in the middle of the room.*)

DAN: There, it that where you want it?

HELEN: (*Surveys the position and points a bit over to the right.*) Move it over there so it will be right in the middle of the room. We'll need four folding chairs, of course.

DAN: (*Goes off stage left and returns with a couple of chairs and places them around the table.*) You know it's always a problem to decide who sits in this room and who gets to sit at the big table in the dining room.

HELEN: A problem? Why?

DAN: Because our daughter, Lori, always complains that she and her husband, Brian, and their son, Fred, have to sit in here while everyone else gets to sit with the grown ups at the big table. (*Points over to the other table in the adjacent room to emphasize his point.*)

HELEN: (*Stops putting placemats on the big table and comes over to listen and then folds her arms across her chest.*) You're just exaggerating.

DAN: You know as well as I do that no one wants to sit out here at the kid's table and Lori always wonders why we punish her.

HELEN: Punish! Who talks about punishment? It's just a card table and it's only a few feet from the rest of us. That's ridiculous. It just can't be that big a deal.

(*DAN turns to go back off stage left and gets the remaining chairs.*)

DAN: I just don't understand. We go through this same discussion every Thanksgiving and Christmas and Mother's Day. Lori gets stuck out here in the den with her family and she feels left out.

HELEN: Yes, and when we put Lori and Susan, our daughter-in-law, at the same table, they always manage to get into a fight about something or other. It doesn't even matter about what. It can be politics, money, immigration, schools. You would think those two really disliked each other, even if they are sisters-in-law.

DAN: Especially because they're sisters-in-law, I would say.

HELEN: And don't forget the tablecloth. Please use the white one with the crocheted border.

(*DAN goes off stage left and returns with the tablecloth.*)

DAN: And what if we put the card table at the end of the big table in the dining room? That way we would be all together in the same room.

HELEN: You know we're not going to start moving all the furniture around just because two grown women can't seem to get along. (*Pauses.*) And use the good placemats out here, too, please. Just like the ones I'm using in the dining room. We don't want anyone to feel left out, do we?

(*DAN goes off stage left and returns with four place mats.*)

DAN: So who's going to be the fourth person out here?

HELEN: What about Steve? He and Fred are cousins, after all. He's quite a bit younger than Lori and Brian, but only a bit older than Fred. I think he might add something to the conversation.

DAN: Steve and Lori don't get along either, even if she is his aunt, plus Fred is at an awkward age when he just doesn't talk to anyone about anything. I don't think any of them like one another, even if they are related. (*Pauses.*) We're sociable people, nice people, with lots of friends and our kids are indifferent or even hostile to each other. It's amazing.

(*HELEN hands DAN the plates.*)

HELEN: Of course they love one another. They're family, right? And families are supposed to get along together through thick and thin, just like us.

DAN: We have had our share of problems, but we're still married. Everyone else is just related. I guess we can't make people love one another or even like one another for that matter, even if they're our children. (*Finishes putting on the glasses.*) Honey, can't we move everyone to the living room and just put the little table at the end of the big table, please? Just this time to see how it goes.

HELEN: No.

DAN: For peace and harmony's sake?

(*HELEN shakes a fork in his direction.*)

HELEN: You talk like we are a bunch of animals fighting in a barnyard. The children may have their differences, but in the end, they all love one another.

DAN: No, dear, they don't. And I shudder to think of what will happen when we are gone, despite our precautions. (*Picks up a couple of forks and begins banging them together like sabers.*) They will fight over every fork, every spoon, every glass and every piece of worthless furniture.

HELEN: No they won't, we've made arrangements. (*Removes the forks from his hands and replaces them on the table and then sits down on one of the chairs while DAN sits down on the adjacent chair.*) What did we do wrong?

DAN: Nothing.

HELEN: But we had to have failed somewhere. Children are supposed to love and support one another. (*Gestures at the table.*) It can't be because of this, being at the big table or the small one, can it?

(*DAN shrugs and reaches out to take HELEN's hand.*)

DAN: Maybe. Maybe we just didn't know which table to use and when.

(*HELEN stands up.*)

HELEN: No. We have always done our best.

(*The doorbell rings. DAN walks over and opens a door stage left. LORI stands there with a bouquet of flowers. She kisses DAN and goes over and kisses HELEN.*)

LORI: Hello, Dad. Hello, Mom. I just thought I'd drop some flowers by for the dinner. (*Glances from the card table to the big table in the living room.*) Let me guess. Brian and Fred and I will be sitting out here at the kid's table again? And perhaps Steve will have to join us?

(*LORI goes over and sits down on one of the folding chairs. HELEN and DAN do the same.*)

HELEN: Don't you think the table looks nice?

LORI: Yes, it looks fine. It's just that it's a little annoying to be stuck out here at the kid's table when the so-called adults are over there at the big table having fun. How do you think that makes me feel? Or Brian or Fred? We feel like the distant relations or more like the adults who never grew up being relegated to the kid's table. (*Stands up and begins gesticulating.*) We appreciate you hosting these family get-togethers. I know it's a lot of time and work and money. But can we sit at the big table? Just for once? Put someone else here for once! Anybody else!

DAN: Don't yell at your mother.

(*LORI sighs and sits down.*)

HELEN: You and your sister-in-law, Susan, don't seem to have much in common. And when you're together at the big table, there's always so much fussing and fighting.

LORI: Much in common? That's a joke! She's always pontificating about child rearing or medicine or some important meeting she's going to. She doesn't talk, she lectures. It's boring and it's annoying. Put them at the little table, just once. Put Susan and my brother here with Steve at this table. Let them be one small happy family out here and the rest of us can sit at the big table. That would solve the problem.

HELEN: But we couldn't.

LORI: Why not? Because you love them and respect them and you don't care about us or what we think? Is that it?

HELEN: Of course not. We love you all. And we want you to love one another. We want a loving family where everyone gets along without fighting or criticizing or yelling.

DAN: Helen, please. Don't upset yourself.

HELEN: I'm not upsetting myself.

(*LORI stands up.*)

LORI: So that's it. I'm the one. I'm the problem child. (*Walks toward the door.*) Okay, we'll sit here in the den at the kid's table again. (*Points to the card table.*) We'll sit here and we'll pretend to love everyone and we won't fight. Is that what you want? (*Checks her watch.*) We'll be back at seven with our good clothes and our best manners.

(*DAN stands up to see her out.*)

DAN: We love you. We love all of our children.

LORI: Yes, just like in Animal Farm. You love all of your children, you just love some more than others.

(*HELEN stands up, knocking her chair over in the process.*)

HELEN: No. It's not like that at all. Some children are just needier than others.

LORI: That's supposed to make me feel better? So do the needier children get sit at the big table or at the kid's table?

(*HELEN begins to answer, but DAN raises his hand.*)

DAN: Don't answer that.

LORI: I can take it. I'm a big girl.

DAN: We love you all, and we look forward to seeing you later this evening. Thank you for bringing the beautiful flowers. It's a lovely gesture and we really appreciate it.

(*LORI opens the door and sees herself out. DAN returns to the table and picks up the overturned chair. DAN and HELEN both sit down.*)

DAN: Can we move this table and put it with the big one now, even if we have to move furniture around?

HELEN: (*Sighs.*) Yes. I think that would be a good idea.

(*DAN takes HELEN's hand. Lights dim to dark.*)

THE END

HANGING BY A THREAD

CAST OF CHARACTERS

CRAIG: Mrs. Helen Hamptons's son. A middle aged, well-dressed man.

ANNE: Mrs. Helen Hampton's daughter. A middle aged woman, with a slightly unkept appearance.

DR. FRANKLIN: The Hampton family physician. A middle aged doctor, dressed in a lab coat.

SETTING

Dr. Franklin's office. There are three chairs and perhaps a desk. The doctor's chair faces the other two. Dr. Franklin is dressed in a tie and white lab coat, not scrubs. He is sitting in a way that he faces the siblings.

CRAIG: (*Talking loudly to ANNE.*) Don't be ridiculous! Dr. Franklin and I are trying to help end mother's useless suffering.

ANNE: (*Jumps up from her chair and starts screaming.*) Stop spouting this drivel! You're both trying to kill her and you know it!

DR. FRANKLIN: (*To ANNE.*) Killing is forbidden by the Hippocratic Oath. I can't kill people, but I can let nature take its course.

ANNE: Nature! What's natural about starvation? What's natural about euthanasia? What's natural about two men ganging up on a helpless, old woman and snuffing out her life?

DR. FRANKLIN: No one is talking about euthanasia.

ANNE: (*Yells at DR. FRANKLIN.*) God! You're just playing God and you're so full of yourself that you don't even see it.

DR. FRANKLIN: Perhaps you're right, but God shows mercy and compassion in the face of suffering. At least I hope he does.

ANNE: Do you? Is killing old ladies showing compassion?

CRAIG: (*To ANNE.*) Would you shut up! You're insulting the doctor and you're insulting me.

ANNE: You! I haven't even started on you. You're nothing more than the sorcerer's apprentice. You don't even have the balls to make the decision yourself. You stir things up and then hide behind Dr. God here. Yes, you're his lapdog, his ball-less little lap dog.

CRAIG: And you have the balls? Is that it? Is that why you're still an unmarried old maid? Because of your balls?

ANNE: Shut up! (*Lunges at CRAIG and begins to pound his chest.*)

(*CRAIG does not resist, but keeps his hands at his sides.*)

ANNE: You nasty arrogant creep! (*Continues to pound CRAIG, but her blows become weaker and weaker.*)

(*ANNE finally stops and CRAIG puts his arms around her. ANNE pushes CRAIG away.*)

ANNE: I'm going out to the waiting room. Call me if you need me.

CRAIG: Anne is mentally and physically exhausted. Mother's got no quality of life and I can't stand to see them this way. We're prolonging their suffering. Do we have to go on with all these tube feedings? Is it some sort of legal thing about stopping them?

DR. FRANKLIN: No, It's not a legal problem and we don't have to continue the feedings, but your sister wants me to keep them going. If that were not the case, we could convert your mother to comfort care status, get her switched to hospice, and stop the feedings. She would dwindle away and die peacefully.

CRAIG: Would that hurt? Would she suffer?

DR. FRANKLIN: No. We think in terms of ourselves. She won't suffer, she'll just dwindle away.

CRAIG: Starving to death? Dying of dehydration?

DR. FRANKLIN: It's not painful. Nature will take its course in someone who can no longer eat on their own. We could just put water down the tube. She would not die of dehydration, but it will prolong the dying process.

CRAIG: Can we do it? Stop the feeding?

DR. FRANKLIN: Anytime. But you and your sister must agree. You can't have one person in the family fighting with another. It's not worth having that kind of disruption and conflict. Your mother would surely not have wanted to be the source of such a terrible controversy between her children. And you don't want a legacy of bitterness to poison your relationship with your sister.

CRAIG: That's already been poisoned if you haven't noticed. But you are right about mother; she certainly wouldn't want us fighting. She never did. *(Looks at DR. FRANKLIN.)* She really wanted us to get along. As kids, we did, you know. We had a lot of fun together. Then something happened as we got older. The more I succeeded in my own life, the more Anne seemed to resent me. She's so bitter now, and full of guilt. And the weird part is that I don't really know why.

DR. FRANKLIN: Anne appears to sincerely care about your mother and her welfare.

CRAIG: Care? I don't know who she thinks she's really caring for? It's like she's afraid to let go of mother. Afraid of some awful void. *(Pauses.)* Am I some sort of monster to want nature to take its course with my mother?

DR. FRANKLIN: I don't think so. But death is final, and no one knows what lies beyond. It's odd, but I've seen believers and non-believers approach death either with dread or total serenity. Their religious feelings didn't seem to matter that much.

CRAIG: And what do you believe, doctor?

DR. FRANKLIN: It doesn't matter what I believe. This is a family decision.

CRAIG: What you believe does matter. You have all this power in you hands, in your pen. You can keep some patients alive and send others to their deaths with a stroke of your pen. Such power must be intoxicating.

DR. FRANKLIN: It's a huge responsibility and an enormous weight. Sometimes I think I know that a patient is doomed and I turn out to be wrong. I took care of this old man one time and I was trying to help the daughter decide whether to put him on a breathing machine or not. He was lying there on the bed between us and I'm trying to convince the daughter not to be aggressive. And he's dying right there in the bed between us.

CRAIG: What did she do?

DR. FRANKLIN: She decided to have him intubated and, against my better judgment, we did it. *(Pauses.)* Two months later he walked out of the hospital. Every time I see him around town in his wheelchair and with his oxygen, I think about trying to convince his daughter to let him die. She refused. And she was right.

CRAIG: You're not God. You can't foresee the future.

DR. FRANKLIN: No, I can't foresee the future. But I do have the power of life and death over people. And sometimes I do feel like God. That's when it takes someone like your sister to drag me back to earth.

CRAIG: So you think that mother is going to wake up and walk around someday like Anne says she will?

DR. FRANKLIN: No, but I can and do make errors in judgment as much as I try to avoid them.

CRAIG: I'm not looking for perfection, just reasonable compassion. Would you talk to my sister again? She's sitting outside in the waiting room.

DR. FRANKLIN: Of course.

CRAIG: I'll bring her back here, even if I have to drag her in.

DR. FRANKLIN: She needs to come in voluntarily. This has to be a family decision.

> (CRAIG goes out and gets ANNE. ANNE comes in and sits down, while CRAIG remains standing in back of the other chair.)

DR. FRANKLIN: Anne, are you all right? You look very tired.

ANNE: I'm fine. I'm really not tired at all. (*Manages a half-hearted smile.*)

DR. FRANKLIN: How many hours of sleep are you getting?

ANNE: Enough. And I appreciate your concern, but this isn't about me. It's about mother, isn't it?

DR. FRANKLIN: Yes, but you don't want to get sick yourself. If you do, who will take care of your mother?

ANNE: Not Craig. That's for sure. He's washed his hands of the problem. (*Looks at CRAIG, then back to DR. FRANKLIN.*) He finds time for his wife, his kids, his job and his charitable boards, but not for his own mother. He just wants to lead his own selfish life and let mother die in some stinking nursing home. Can you believe such ingratitude?

DR. FRANKLIN: Perhaps Craig's not as strong as you?

ANNE: Strong? No, Craig's weak and spineless and heartless.

DR. FRANKLIN: That's very harsh. Don't you think Craig deserves more credit than that?

ANNE: Harsh? What would you say if your sibling left you to make all the decisions, to do all the work?

DR. FRANKLIN: Has Craig really done that? Or do you just disagree with his conclusions? Maybe you ought to give Craig a chance. It can't be easy for him either.

ANNE: Easy? Who's got the cushy job and the gorgeous, devoted wife, and the brilliant, well-mannered children? Craig's a spoiled brat. And now I'm the one doing everything for mother.

DR. FRANKLIN: Perhaps you're being too hard on yourself and on Craig?

ANNE: Mother's worth it. She raised us almost single handed. Dad spent most of the time away with his job. He died when I was only twelve. After that, mother did it all. She worked, kept house, helped with homework and never missed a softball game. She slaved so Craig and I could go to college. She's a saint. That's all. She's a saint. And saints don't deserve to be abandoned like old, sick dogs. *(Glares at CRAIG, then looks back to DR. FRANKLIN.)* Dad let her down, Craig wants to let her down, but I'm not going to. *(Pauses.)* Do you think she's suffering?

DR. FRANKLIN: I don't think so.

ANNE: Do you think she feels pain?

DR. FRANKLIN: I think she can feel pain, but she probably doesn't recognize it like we do.

ANNE: How can you tell for sure?

DR. FRANKLIN: There's no way to be absolutely sure.

ANNE: I would hate it if she were having pain. I would hate myself for causing it.

DR. FRANKLIN: Why would you hate yourself?

ANNE: I caused mother so much pain for so long. I said such hateful things to her when I was growing up. I do feel guilty, but it would kill me if I were just doing all of this for my own selfish reasons. Do you think I'm selfish, doctor?

DR. FRANKLIN: No, I don't think you're selfish. I think you suffer seeing your mother like this. I think your head tells you one thing while your heart tells you something else. I think you need to put your head and heart in harmony.

ANNE: Put them in harmony. That sounds easy, but it's not. At least not for me. *(Pauses and sighs.)*

DR. FRANKLIN: Your mother hasn't shown any signs of improvement over the last three months, even after we put in the feeding tube. In fact, I find her less responsive.

ANNE: Will she ever get better?

DR. FRANKLIN: No, she won't. What you see is what you get.

ANNE: I've read about these cases where someone's been in a coma for years and then wakes up and asks for a Coke. Why not mother?

DR. FRANKLIN: (*Pauses.*) She's not going to wake up. She is not going to get better. She will get pneumonia or a urinary tract infection or bed sores or God knows what other complication. Every patient in her clinical condition gets deathly ill, it just depends on when. Then, ultimately they die.

ANNE: When?

DR. FRANKLIN: I don't know. Weeks? Months? Years?

CRAIG: This could go on for years?

DR. FRANKLIN: With excellent medical care, yes.

CRAIG: (*To ANNE.*) We can't do that to her. We just can't let her sit and rot for years.

ANNE: We? You speak for both us now? (*To DR. FRANKLIN.*) If she were your mother, what would you do?

DR. FRANKLIN: A doctor shouldn't ever treat his own family. I can't answer that question.

ANNE: So if you can't treat your own mother, what if she were a perfect stranger?

DR. FRANKLIN: I'd stop the feedings, put her under hospice care, and continue making her as comfortable as medically possible. (*Pauses and sighs. Speaks to ANNE.*) I see dozens of these patients in the nursing homes. They get started on tube feedings and then they may live for years. Their muscles contract and atrophy so the patients get all twisted up and deformed. They can't talk. They can't move. But they can feel pain. It breaks my heart to see people like that month after month, year after year. Someday there won't be enough nursing home beds to hold us all. (*Pauses.*) But we have hospice agencies. They give comfort care to end-stage patients. They don't force feedings. They don't send the patients back and forth to the hospital. They can help your mother die painlessly and with dignity.

ANNE: Die with dignity? That's still death, isn't it?

DR. FRANKLIN: Yes, it is still death.

ANNE: And what gives you or Craig or me the right to choose between life and death for my mother?

DR. FRANKLIN: Because your mother can't decide anymore.

ANNE: So doesn't that make us all the more responsible? Shouldn't we be all the more certain that we are not just snuffing out a life because it is inconvenient, or expensive, or just unnecessary?

CRAIG: Please! Get off your moral high horse and look at reality down here. Mother's a vegetable, not a person. She's a plant that we're giving food and water to so she continues to survive for our own selfish reasons.

ANNE: Selfish! Who's selfish here? You, the one who can't stand to see mother suffer? Or me, who has the courage and conviction to stand by her in her most vulnerable hour? (*Stands up and starts yelling.*) I'm not selfish, you are! Both of you men sitting here are talking about a living, breathing human being as if she were a piece of meat. I can't take it. I can't take it any more. (*Starts to cry.*)

(*CRAIG gets up and takes ANNE in his arms. ANNE resists only weakly, and then continues to sob as CRAIG pats her back.*)

CRAIG: Look at yourself. You're worn out. You're exhausted. You're going to die too if you keep going like this and I can't stand to lose you both at the same time. You're the only family I have and I do care about you. I want you to be happy, too.

ANNE: (*Backs up a little and looks up at CRAIG.*) I don't want to lose mother.

CRAIG: She'll still be here. (*Points to ANNE's heart, then his own.*) In your heart and in my heart.

ANNE: (*Manages a weak laugh.*) You always had a knack for such sentimental drivel.

CRAIG: And you have the hardest head of anyone I know, except perhaps Mom.

ANNE: As hard as your heart?

CRAIG: You're head's harder by far.

DR. FRANKLIN: (*Looks at his watch. Approaches the siblings.*) I'm sorry to push things along, but have you reached some sort of decision here?

ANNE: (*Turns to CRAIG.*) Can we make a decision now?

DR. FRANKLIN: It's yours to make, Anne. Not mine or your mother's.

ANNE: (*Speaks to CRAIG.*) Am I really being so selfish, so sanctimonious, so unreasonable to want her to live?

CRAIG: No, you're not selfish or sanctimonious or unreasonable. I just think you're wrong.

ANNE: (*Laughs despite herself.*) You really are something. (*Pauses.*) I have an awful feeling that mother is hanging to life by a thread and we're going to cut it.

CRAIG: Yes, we're going to cut the thread to set her free. It's holding her back from God.

DR. FRANKLIN: Does this mean we can stop the tube feedings and continue with comfort measures only?

CRAIG: Anne?

ANNE: (*To CRAIG.*) I'm tired. I'm exhausted and I'm ready to see it end. (*Turns to DR. FRANKLIN.*) I agree. Let's go with hospice and comfort care only.

DR. FRANKLIN: Comfort care only. No food. No water. No antibiotics. (*Looks at ANNE and CRAIG and pauses.*) Now you have to decide whether you want to keep her at home or put her in a nursing home.

ANNE: No! No nursing home, please.

DR. FRANKLIN: (*To ANNE.*) Hospice nurses can provide their services in the nursing home.

ANNE: No! No nursing home. I can bend, but that would break me. (*Turns to CRAIG and clutches his hand.*) Craig, I promised her she'd never have to go into a nursing home.

CRAIG: She's already gone away. Her mind's gone and her body's going. Nursing home, home, what difference does it make at this point?

ANNE: It makes a difference to me. I'd like to continue treating her at home. Please let me have that concession. It won't affect either of you. Let me at least have that small concession.

CRAIG: It's already so hard on you trying to take care of mother. It's wearing you out. It's a 24 hour a day job, seven days a week.

ANNE: That's okay, Craig. I know the consequences and I'm willing to accept them. Please let me keep her at home.

CRAIG: (*To DR. FRANKLIN.*) It's okay with me to continue treating her at home if Anne insists. She knows what she's getting into and she knows what it's doing to her. I respect her for that, even if I don't agree.

DR. FRANKLIN: You'll both have to sign a DNR, a Do Not Resuscitate form.

ANNE: No resuscitation?

DR. FRANKLIN: No chest compressions or intubation when she stops breathing and her heart stops. We just keep her comfortable when that happens.

ANNE: She won't suffer, will she?

DR. FRANKLIN: No, I promise. She does not have to suffer and she will not.

ANNE: Please, give me your word. I can't stand the thought of her suffering.

DR. FRANKLIN: You have my word. She will not suffer.

THE END

THE INHERITANCE

CAST OF CHARACTERS

KAREN: She is a middle aged woman, sister to Debbie. She is dressed in casual clothing, nothing stylish or distinguished. Her hair and make up are minimal.

DEBBIE: Also a middle aged woman, sister to Karen. She is well dressed in professional clothing. Her hair is styled and she wears noticeable but tasteful make up.

SETTING

The set is made up of two card tables and two simple chairs. They are separated by five or more feet to create a sense of physical separation.

(*The two women walk on stage. Each is carrying a cardboard box with their name "KAREN" and "DEBBIE" printed in large, black letters on the side. The boxes must be exactly the same size. DEBBIE puts her box on one table and KAREN puts hers on the another. They may be seated or standing as determined by the director.*)

DEBBIE: Well, let's see what Mama decided to leave us.

KAREN: (*Looks over at DEBBIE.*) I think your box looks bigger than mine?

DEBBIE: (*Shrugs and looks heavenward.*) No it's not. They're exactly the same size. You're always worried about not getting enough. Greedy and needy, that's what you are, just greedy and needy. You always were and you always will be.

KAREN: For heaven's sake, Mama's hardly cold and we've already started fighting. It's shameful. Besides, it was always you who wanted all the attention. Debbie this, Debbie that. Debbie as valedictorian, Debbie graduating *Summa Cum Laude* from Tulane. I bet she gave you a mirror just to look at yourself.

DEBBIE: (*Ignores KAREN turns back to her box. Pulls out a woolen scarf.*) This looks like Grandma's old scarf. (*Sniffs it.*) It smells like Grandma, too. (*Drops it on the table.*) What on earth am I going to do with a woolen scarf in Orlando?

KAREN: Maybe Mama gave it to you because you're so cold hearted. It might warm you up. (*Pulls out a dinner bell from her box and rings it.*) Dinner's ready!

DEBBIE: Dinner. (*Pauses.*) My God, how I hated our family sitting around the dinner table and pretending we liked each other and that there weren't any problems. I think Mama thought that food would somehow dissolve all the secrets, lies and unhappiness. Yes, *bon appetit!* (*Pulls out a large wooden ladle.*) You've got to be kidding!

KAREN: (*Looks over and laughs.*) That's Mama's all right, her old gumbo spoon. She got that from some guy down in Opelousas. I remember when she bought it. You would have thought it was some magic wand. She never used anything else to make a roux. Maybe she wanted you to start cooking a little.

DEBBIE: (*Clacks the wooden spoon down on the table.*) Fat chance! I pay people to do that now. And I never thought that homemade food was going to make everything right. I don't care if it was a gumbo or *étouffée* or *jambalaya*. And don't get me started on those stinky little crawfish. What a mess! (*She looks back at KAREN's box and waves her hands in the air.*) Okay, what else have you got in there?

KAREN: (*Pulls out a disheveled doll.*) Doris! (*She hugs the doll.*) Mama gave me this doll when I was six years old. I thought it was the most amazing doll in the world. (*Holds the doll back and examines it.*) I only got tired of it when I reached 14 and started thinking about boys. Maybe I should have stuck to Doris instead of getting pregnant at 18. (*Looks at the doll.*) It looks so old and raggedy. I thought it got thrown away years ago. (*Pauses and looks at the doll.*)

DEBBIE: (*Reaches in and pulls out a hunting knife.*) Wow! It's Papa's old hunting knife. Now that's a sentimental gift. I wonder if it still cuts like it did. (*Examines the edge and then stabs it in the direction of her sister.*) That was the sharpest knife I ever saw. Maybe this will cut through a few problems. (*Waves the knife in the air.*)

KAREN: Maybe that's why Mama gave it to you, to cut through your problems. She was always worried about you not staying married and having all those bad husbands and boyfriends. She wanted you to have children and a stable home. I guess she even saw your financial success as a problem, too.

DEBBIE: (*Throws the knife down on the table with a clatter.*) Who's talking about problems? I don't have a loser husband and three wild kids. I'm not stuck in nowhere-ville in a dead end minimum wage job with no prospects. I don't look like somebody's cleaning lady. Maybe you need this knife more than I do? Maybe you can just slit your wrists and get out of this hell hole. (*Looks over at KAREN who looks shocked. A long silence follows.*) Sorry. That was over the top. (*Pauses.*) What else have you got in there anyway?

KAREN: (*Reaches in and pulls out a photo album.*) A scrapbook. (*Opens it up.*) No, it's a photo album. (*Puts it on the table and begins flipping through it. Starts looking somewhere in the middle.*)

DEBBIE: (*Wanders over to KAREN's table and looks at the album as KAREN turns the pages.*) I didn't even know she had a photo album.

KAREN: Here's our visit to Disneyworld. There you are standing next to Snow White. You were looking up at her like she was some magical princess.

DEBBIE: (*Examines the picture.*) Right! Look at those red lips and black hair and laced up boobs. Snow White had so much make up on she looked like an Orlando whore.

KAREN: And look at you. You were barely 13 and you already dressed like a slut. Look at that mini-skirt and skin-tight tank top. Who really looked like the prostitute?

DEBBIE: Takes one to know one.

KAREN: Who slept with three different boys in high school and I don't know how many through college? We never saw the same guy twice, not even your husbands.

DEBBIE: Well, at least I was smart enough not to get knocked up before leaving high school. At least I went to college and graduated. (*Swings her arms around.*) And I got out of this dump.

KAREN: Yes, I am still here, but at least I'm doing some good for someone. I raise three kids and take care of my husband, work in a day care, and still find time to volunteer for the PTA and Salvation Army and the Food Bank. (*Points an accusing finger.*) And what do you do besides make a bunch of money and jump from bed to bed with your succession of rich, pretentious, professional dickheads?

DEBBIE: Dick's yes, just what you want and your philandering husband doesn't give you anymore.

KAREN: (*Taken aback.*) How do you know that?

DEBBIE: I saw your husband flirting with every available younger woman at Mama's wake. You can't tell me you didn't see what he was doing.

KAREN: (*Hangs her head.*) I saw. But I still have my own children, plus the kids at the daycare, my friends, and my church.

DEBBIE: Friends! Daycare! Church! You can put all of your friend's intellects into a thimble. And half of your daycare children will end up on drugs, in prison or both. And a few lucky ones might get a job on an oil rig somewhere.

(Both remain silent for a long while. KAREN turns the page of the album.)

KAREN: And here you are on that trip to Cancun with Mama and me. Do you even remember the trip? Or were you so drunk that you can't remember anything at all? I lost count of all your margaritas.

DEBBIE: I paid for you and Mama to go on that trip. It was my gift to both of you. It was so we could bond a little, you ungrateful bitch!

KAREN: The only thing you bonded with was Tequila. And you're the bitch! A rich, bitch witch!

DEBBIE: *(Raises her hand to strike her sister, but stops in midair. Speaks softly.)* Rich, bitch, witch.

KAREN: *(Nods.)* Yes.

DEBBIE: *(Sighs.)* I didn't know you were a poet. *(Lowers her hand and starts to laugh. And then shakes her head and turns a few more pages of the album.)* Look at this one. We were on that trip to Yosemite, before Papa died. Do you remember?

KAREN: *(Nods and smoothes out her dress, and then bends down to look more closely at the picture.)* How could I forget? We stood on that mountain and looked over the valley at Half Dome in the afternoon light. It glowed like a lump of pure gold. It was beautiful, magical. Papa looked so happy. You'd thought he might have invented the place, just to impress us. It was so gorgeous, so peaceful. It was like an open air cathedral where you couldn't help but be respectful. We didn't have a single fight on that trip.

DEBBIE: And remember that night in the Alawahnee Lodge down in Yosemite Valley? Remember that dance party with fiddles and a banjo and an accordion?

KAREN: Yes, of course. Papa taught us both how to dance the polka. And he danced with each of us over and over, swinging us around like rag dolls all evening long. He even danced with Mama until she was completely out of breath. It was unbelievable.

DEBBIE: Do you remember how?

KAREN: How to polka? Sure. You wanna try?

DEBBIE: I haven't danced in years. (*Looks at KAREN skeptically.*) This isn't a trick, is it?

KAREN: No. (*Raises her arms.*) Come on, it's like swimming. You never really forget.

> (*DEBBIE takes KAREN's arms and they begin to dance to the music of "Beer Barrel Polka." The twirl around and do a few turns. They sing the refrain "Roll out the barrel; we'll have a barrel of fun" a couple of times as they dance. KAREN turns DEBBIE under her arm and the music fades. They both laugh and catch their breaths. DEBBIE returns to her box as does KAREN.*)

KAREN: (*Reaches in and pulls out a Teddy Bear.*) I'll be darned. It's Peter.

DEBBIE: Peter? I thought it was Charlie or something like that.

KAREN: No, Charlie was my first boyfriend. (*Caresses the bear.*) Papa gave me this bear when I was around seven. He brought it back from some sort of trip, maybe to Germany. Do you remember?

DEBBIE: Yes, I remember. That was when he told Mama about his first affair. Do you remember that? All the screaming and yelling, it was horrible. I thought I was going to cry myself to death.

KAREN: I wonder why Mama gave me the scrapbook and not you? And why I got four things and you only got three?

DEBBIE: I guess she just loved you more. (*Smiles.*)

KAREN: Or maybe she gave me more things because she thought I needed it, like you said. Because I'm needy and greedy.

DEBBIE: (*Shrugs her shoulders.*) Or maybe she loved us both just the same. (*Looks over at KAREN's box.*) She just gave you an extra gift. (*Returns to her box on the table and puts the scarf, the spoon and the knife back in the box.*) Well, it's all going to Goodwill. I don't want any of it. (*Picks up the box.*) I think it's time to let go of it all. Let's simplify or lives, don't you think?

KAREN: (*Hugs the doll and puts it in back in the box along with the Teddy bear.*) Hell's bells. (*Rings the bell and tosses it into the box as well. She picks up the photo album.*) This too? It's got a lot of sentimental value.

(*A piece of paper falls out of the photo album.*)

DEBBIE: (*Walks over and picks it up and reads it.*) "To both of my girls with all my love. Thanks for the memories."

KAREN: The album was for both of us, not just me.

(*They embrace, and then separate.*)

DEBBIE: Yes. (*Smiles.*) But it still needs to go to Goodwill. Let them throw it away.

KAREN: (*Hesitates.*) I would like my children to know what their grandparents looked like. What if I keep just one picture?

DEBBIE: Keep the whole album if you want to.

KAREN: I just need one. (*Takes one picture out of the album and puts the rest in the box.*) The rest can go to Goodwill.

DEBBIE: Which one did you keep?

KAREN: The happy one, Yosemite.

(KAREN and DEBBIE *pick up their boxes and walk back where they entered. They exit. Lights dim to dark.*)

THE END

KATRINA'S WAKE

CAST OF CHARACTERS

DR. CAROL BERGERON: Female physician at St. Rita Hospital, New Orleans after Hurricane Katrina. She is dressed in a soiled lab coat over dirty scrubs.

NURSE CODY: Male nurse at St. Rita Hospital, New Orleans. He is dressed in dirty scrubs.

JEAN STAFFORD: Female patient at St. Rita. She suffers from end stage emphysema and can hardly breathe. She struggles with an oxygen mask which she takes off and on to speak.

SETTING

The set is a stark, dirty hospital room. There are a couple of chairs and a hospital bed. The patient is hooked up to an oxygen tank and an IV. The patient's sheets are soiled. Light may be filtering in from a high window, which casts a shadow on the floor but is too high to see out. There is a trash can overflowing with medical waste and trash.

STAFFORD: (*Gasps for breath with every sentence while holding off the mask to speak.*) I'm having a terrible time, doc. Can you give me more oxygen or put me back on that breathing machine or anything to help me out? I don't want to die in this filthy place.

BERGERON: There's no power to run the ventilators. (*Points to the oxygen tank.*) This is the last oxygen tank in the building. And Cody here is the only nurse left to help. Your IV fluids are almost out and all I could salvage from the pharmacy was this last bottle of morphine.

(*Gun shots and shouting offstage.*)

CODY: Listen to them gunshots. They sound pretty close.

BERGERON: They're probably coming from the pharmacy upstairs. Armed looters are all over the place looking for drugs.

STAFFORD: Are we safe here?

BERGERON: There's no food, no medicine, nothing left to steal around here except this. (*Holds up the morphine vial.*) Dirty laundry, trash, flies, mosquitoes. Yeah, I guess we're safe, if you can call it that.

CODY: Safe? That's debatable. (*To STAFFORD.*) Armed crackheads are shootin' the place up and the doc here wants to give you a medication that might kill you. That doesn't sound too safe to me.

BERGERON: (*To Cody.*) What are saying? I am the doctor and you are the nurse. Who's in charge here, anyway?

CODY: In charge? That's a joke! There's nobody in charge, doc. Haven't you noticed? I know I'm supposed to shut up and follow orders. But that's in normal times. This is chaos. This is a free-for-all and I can and will express my opinions, however blunt, to Mrs. Stafford. What are you goin' to do about it anyway? Fire me? Report me to my higher ups? (*Pauses.*) In case you haven't noticed, our Director of Nursing and our CEO both flew the coop. (*Back to STAFFORD.*) We've been abandoned in this hell hole where we're all probably goin' to die.

BERGERON: Would you shut up and stop upsetting the patient! I am still the doctor here whether you respect my authority or not. (*Turns to STAFFORD.*) Mrs. Stafford, what little lungs you have left are filled with infection that's causing pain. I have some morphine and I'm only planning ahead if things get any worse.

STAFFORD: How can they get worse? (*Gasps and winces.*) It hurts when I breathe. (*Looks around and sniffs.*) Can you smell that stench? Dear God. (*Looks at the ceiling.*) Look at the drops coming off the ceiling. It looks like urine. (*Waves away flies.*) This pain, this heat and humidity, they're killing me. It's already hell in here. I'm suffocating. (*Grabs the mask and gasps for breath.*) For God's sake, isn't anyone coming to save us?

BERGERON: The city's flooded. There's no way in or out. It's not even safe to come in by air. Thugs are shooting at the rescue helicopters. (*Holds up the vials of medicine and shows them to STAFFORD.*) This is morphine. It disconnects your mind from your body. You would feel better immediately, without a sense of suffocation. It will not make your breathing any better, but you will be pain-free and comfortable.

STAFFORD: Comfort. My God. (*Gasps and wheezes.*) That does sound nice. (*Takes BERGERON's hand.*) What's your first name?

BERGERON: Carol.

STAFFORD: May I call you Carol?

BERGERON: Of course.

STAFFORD: Thank you, Carol. (*Gasps and wheezes.*) Please tell me, do I have any chance of getting out of this place alive? And even if I did, would I ever get better?

BERGERON: (*Feels STAFFORD's forehead*). Mrs. Stafford, you are burning with fever. Your breathing is getting worse and even if you survived this place, your underlying lung condition is bad and will continue to deteriorate with time. I can't tell you for sure when you will die. Only God can do that.

CODY: The IV's out. (*Takes it down and walks to the trash can to throw it away.*) Listen to those guns out there. It's crazy. And this heat. I'm meltin'. Is there any water left? Any cigarettes? (*Rummages around the room, even looking in the trash.*)

BERGERON: Everything's gone and you want a cigarette? If you smoke one with Mrs. Stafford's oxygen on, you'd blow us all up. Even if you found a cigarette, I forbid you from smoking. Don't put all of our lives in any more danger than they are already in.

CODY: Danger? Look who's talkin'. I might pose a theoretical danger from smokin' and blowin' us up, but you're standin' there with a fatal dose of morphine in your hand. Who's the danger to who? (*Pauses.*) I thought docs took an oath not to kill people.

BERGERON: (*To CODY.*) You just won't shut up, will you? This discussion is between Mrs. Stafford and me.

CODY: Really? And the family? Don't they get a say?

BERGERON: The family! What family? Not one member of her family stayed with Ms. Stafford. Not one. They all cleared out when the water started rising. And why shouldn't they? They have a right to leave. It's our responsibility to stay here with the patients.

STAFFORD: (*Pulls off her masks and speak in gasps.*) I can't expect my family to risk their lives for me. (*Gasps and wheezes.*) They're young. They have their whole lives ahead of them. I'm just a worn out old woman who smoked herself to death. (*Gasps.*) I don't want to die, but I think death's coming for me whether I want it or not. Carol. (*Takes BERGERON's hand.*) Maybe you can just make it easier.

CODY: (*To BERGERON.*) Now don't you be lettin' this old lady push you into somethin' we're all goin' to regret. I'm a witness to all this, doc, and I'm sure as hell not puttin' my license on the line for some sick old patient, even if she is nice. (*Points to STAFFORD.*)

STAFFORD: (*To BERGERON.*) Yes, my family did leave. But you both stayed. You didn't have to stay and you did. (*Gasps.*) Why didn't you leave? Why don't you leave now?

BERGERON: We have a professional obligation to stay. But we also want to.

STAFFORD: (*To CODY.*) Even for a used up sick old lady like me?

CODY: (*To STAFFORD.*) I got my obligations, too. We're not supposed to abandon patients, even when they smoked themselves to death.

BERGERON: (*Drops STAFFORD's hand and points to CODY in an accusing way.*) Cody, I know you're a good nurse and a good person. So please show some compassion. Mrs. Stafford doesn't need insults or lectures, she needs compassion.

CODY: How dare you talk about compassion with a syringe full of morphine in your hand! That's insane, doc, and you know it.

STAFFORD: No! It's insane of you both to stay here and try and help me. (*Gasps and wheezes.*) I can't get out of here. I can't even take a deep breath. My God, it hurts every time I breathe.

CODY: (*Shakes the tank.*) That's it. The oxygen tank is empty.

BERGERON: What do you want me to do, Mrs. Stafford? I don't know what's right, but I think you are dying. Everything's gone now, even the oxygen. I have nothing left to offer but this. (*Shows the syringe.*)

STAFFORD: Call me Jean. (*Gasps. No longer on oxygen and is clearly getting worse quickly.*)

STAFFORD: Give me peace, Carol. I want relief. I can't breathe anymore. I can't stand the pain. I can't stand the feeling of suffocation. If I can't live, then please let me die without pain and with dignity, not struggling for the last bit of air. Help me!

CODY: Don't do it, doc. Think about Kevorkian. He went to prison and he's still rottin' there. They took him away for doin' the same thing and you'll end up in a prison hell hole like him. The lawyers will be after you, me, this hospital and anyone else they think has any money. Think about that. You know I'm right.

BERGERON: Where are those lawyers now? Do you see any lawyers? Are there any damn lawyers here to help this suffering woman?

CODY: No. There aren't any lawyers here now. But they will come and they'll be thicker than the flies and mosquitoes in this filthy place. (*Pauses.*) I may not snitch on you, Dr. Bergeron, but I'm not goin' to prison for perjury. If someone asks me under oath, then, by God, I'll answer with the truth. And you'll go to prison, too, just like Kevorkian and none of your fancy colleagues in their fancy homes and cars will come to your defense. You'll be treated like another mercy killer, nailed to the cross of justice just like Kevorkian whether you deserve it or not.

BERGERON: I'm no Kevorkian. And we're not in the comfort of some terminal patient's living room. We're in hell in case you haven't noticed. (*Swings her arms around in a wide gesture.*)

STAFFORD: Please give me the morphine. (*Gasps and wheezs.*) I want to live, but I can't. You proposed morphine and now I'm begging you to give it to me. I pray to God that my family will understand. I'm finished. At least give me comfort, Carol. I beg you. Give me peace.

BERGERON: (*Approaches the IV line with the syringe, but hesitates.*) Jean, I don't know if this is the right thing to do. I don't even know if it's peace, but it's all I have. (*Pulls back and looks at JEAN.*) Will God forgive me if I'm wrong?

CODY: No, doc, he won't, and neither will your armchair quarterback doctor colleagues, all comfy in their dry, air-conditioned homes. Doc, you didn't go to medical school to do this. You know it's wrong. Don't throw your life away on somethin' like this.

BERGERON: (*To CODY.*) Something? No. Someone. And you don't have to participate if you don't want to. I take full responsibility for everything. I may be wrong, but I have to relieve suffering. Turn your back on us. It's okay.

CODY: You bet I'm turnin' my back. I'm not going to the slammer for someone who's dyin' of emphysema and pneumonia anyway. (*Turns his back and crosses his arms.*)

STAFFORD: Give it to me, Carol. Quit arguing and give it to me. . . NOW! (*Gasps and then speaks to CODY.*) And you, nurse, you're a coward who can't even help an old lady and a doctor who needs you.

BERGERON: (*To CODY.*) You have always had an important role to play in patient care and you have never been afraid to speak your mind about it.

CODY: (*Whips around to face the doctor.*) Like now, doc? To defend the patient. To defend life in the face of doctor-assisted death.

BERGERON: Yes, like now. (*Holds up the syringe and the vial in a communion-like gesture, then looks at STAFFORD who stares up at her.*) Would you forgive me if I didn't give this morphine? Would God?

STAFFORD: I forgive you whatever you do. I can't speak for God, but I want to go to him now and I'll tell him what you did for me. God'll have to decide about you later.

(*More gunshots. Glass breaking.*)

CODY: Jesus, that's right down the hall. You can smell the gunshots. They'll be here any minute.

BERGERON: If they get in here, they'll take this morphine. It's now or never. (*To STAFFORD.*) Jean, look me in the eyes. You are tired and sick, but you have to help me. You have to be the strong one. (*To CODY.*) Hold her hand, please.

CODY: Does that make me an accomplice?

STAFFORD: No, (*Gasps*) just a decent person.

(*CODY takes STAFFORD's hand.*)

BERGERON: Ready?

STAFFORD: Ready. (*Pulls BERGERON down close to her.*) I forgive you. (*Reaches up and touches the BERGERON's forehead. Gasps.*) And I won't tell anyone but God. (*Smiles and falls back on her bed.*) Please, inject it.

BERGERON: You'll feel sleepy. You won't feel pain. You won't feel short of breath. You'll feel peaceful. It's not meant to shorten your life, but it may. (*Injects the syringe.*)

STAFFORD: Oh, that's better. (*Sighs and looks at BERGERON.*) Carol, I thought you were going to talk me to death and that's no way to go. (*Slumps down.*) Thank you both. (*Dies.*)

CODY: (*Pulls the sheet over STAFFORD's head*). Nice lady. (*Looks around at the room.*) Horrible place to die. But she was lyin' about not tellin' anyone.

BERGERON: She's no liar. She was a wonderful woman. Someone we can admire. She's a hero who took responsibility to the bitter end. (*Looks back at CODY.*) What are you talking about, anyway?

CODY: She's got those drugs in her system, doc. And when the coroner gets a hold of her body, her blood will scream out at you from beyond the grave. You know I'm right.

BERGERON: Perhaps you are right, but there's nothing we can do about that now. (*Crosses herself and then points to the empty vials and syringe.*) Would you please throw this vial and syringe away?

CODY: Not me! I'm not touchin' that stuff with a ten foot pole.

(*More gunshots. More glass breading and shouting. The sound is much closer..*)

CODY: God, that's close. They must be right outside the door.

BERGERON: (*Throws the empty vial and syringe into the trash can.*) We need to get out of here. If we go up the back stairwell, we might make it to the roof. Follow me.

CODY: No way, doc. I'm goin' take my chances through the flooded lobby.

(*BERGERON leaves. CODY looks back at the corpse. He tucks in the dangling sheet and crosses himself as he leaves.*)

CODY: Poor lady. Damn Katrina. God have mercy on us all. *(Leaves in a different direction. Lights out.)*

THE END

LIVES

CAST OF CHARACTERS

ROBERT VASE: CEO of a small, struggling hospital in rural Louisiana. He is dressed in a tie and button-down shirt. His pants are pressed and his shoes shined. He speaks with a slight French accent.

ACHILLE PIERRE: Local country doctor, Robert's friend. He wears a wrinkled lab coat. His shoes are not shined. He may or may not have a tie. He speaks with a slight French accent.

ALEX TOURNEVISSE. A well-dressed corporate representative. No regional accent.

SETTING

They are in Robert's office at the hospital. There is a desk and a couple of chairs. There may be a cheesy hunting picture or Cajun cottage scene on the wall.

SCENE I

ACHILLE: No! No! No! I don't agree! It's not right. And it's not legal.

ROBERT: It's the only way out, Achille. We have been hemorrhaging enrolled lives from our Deep South Health Maintenance Organization, our glorious HMO. Every month more people leave the HMO than sign up. (*Holds up a letter.*) I'm already getting menacing letters from Corporate. Listen to this. (*Takes a letter and reads.*) "Given your declining enrollments at the Tunica-Biloxi division of the Deep South HMO, we may be forced to close your institution. Only a drastic improvement in patient numbers will avert a regrettable decision for closure." Etcetera, etcetera. (*Collapses in his executive chair.*) They're going to close us if we don't get our numbers up. The only way to increase enrollees is to sign up the dead.

ACHILLE: I'm not going to sign up dead people! Maybe we should close this place down?

ROBERT: Are you crazy? Close this hospital we've both spent our life creating? You've got to be crazy.

ACHILLE: No, I'm not. But I am exhausted. You got me into this mess in the first place. (*Looks over at the liquor cabinet.*) I need a drink.

(*ROBERT offers ACHILLE a drink.*)

ACHILLE: You told me by signing up with your damn HMO that I would be earning more money while seeing fewer patients. (*Pauses.*) You lied! Every deathly ill old maid and widow in this parish signed up to see me. They all want to come in three times a month instead of every three months. I've doubled my paperwork, extended my hours, and earn less than before. You lied!

ROBERT: Let's just say I miscalculated. I thought you were going to get fat monthly checks for doing nothing.

ACHILLE: Well, you did miscalculate . . . badly.

ROBERT: For that, I am truly sorry. But we can't let our personal misfortunes cloud our obligations to the people of Tunica-Biloxi Parish. They need our hospital. They need you! I'm asking you to do this for the good of our parish.

ACHILLE: No! You are asking me to do this for you, personally, because it will save your sorry ass.

ROBERT: And keep our hospital open.

ACHILLE: (*Takes a drink.*) Yes, and keep this hospital open. (*Takes another drink.*) Okay, so how does your latest brainchild work?

ROBERT: Simple, we sign up dead people. (*Waits.*) It increases the enrollment to the HMO without increasing the costs.

ACHILLE: And when no one pays for their enrollment, what happens? The dead can't pay, can they? Or have you figured that one out yet, too?

ROBERT: That's the beauty. It doesn't matter. (*Pauses. Shows a little black book.*) I've got a little black book here filled with the names, dates of birth and social security numbers of dead people. As long as they aren't consuming my hospital resources or your time, it doesn't make any difference. (*Holds up a black book.*) The cemeteries are full of potential enrollees. (*Reads.*) Henry Doucet, Marie Lemoine, Jeremy Ponthieux, Charles Soileau, Matilda Villemarette. It's endless, I tell you. It's a miracle. This book and the names it contains is our salvation.

ACHILLE: And do you think that Corporate is so stupid? Don't you think someone will figure out that you are signing up dead people?

ROBERT: By the time they get suspicious, we will have enrolled a lot of new real people and we'll be able to purge the lists. Yes, it's tricky. Yes, it's unorthodox, but we need our hospital. I need my job. And you need to lighten up.

ACHILLE: All the way to prison?

ROBERT: Who said anything about prison?

ACHILLE: Illegal activity always leads to prison sooner or later.

ROBERT: No one is going to prison, especially in Louisiana. I tell you, it's just a temporary expedient to get Corporate off my back. (*Pauses.*) If you don't want to do it for the hospital or for the people, then just do it for me. Do it for your sister, my wife. She doesn't want me to be unemployed any more than you. I swear it's just temporary, cross my heart and hope to die.

ACHILLE: I'll do it for you and for my sister, even though I warned her not to marry a good for nothing hospital administrator like you.

ROBERT: (*Hugs ACHILLE.*) I knew you'd help me out and you won't regret it, I swear. (*Serves himself a drink and raises his glass.*) Here's to our new lives for the Deep South HMO. To their health! *Santé*!

ACHILLE: *Santé*? That's ridiculous. They're dead.

ROBERT: Okay, to our health!

SCENE II

(*ROBERT is seated at the desk in his office. He is flipping through his black book. He looks up at ACHILLE, who enters into his office.*)

ROBERT: Ah, Achille, it's so nice to see you. Thanks so much for dropping by.

ACHILLE: What now? Not enough dead people to sign up for the HMO?

ROBERT: Oh no, plenty of dead people. The obituaries are full and my black book of the dead is almost full as well.

ACHILLE: So what do you need me to do now?

ROBERT: (*Gets up and puts his arm around ACHILLE's shoulders.*) You have been our savior, our number one regional HMO doctor.

ACHILLE: With a bunch of dead lives?

ROBERT: And live ones, too.

ACHILLE: Yes, and those are the ones that are killing me. Mrs. D'Autremont came in four times last week only. It's amazing. I didn't think you could invent that many diseases.

ROBERT: She won't be coming in any more. Didn't you see?

ACHILLE: See what?

ROBERT: Here. (*Picks up a newspaper and shows it to Achille.*) Her name is in the obituaries.

ACHILLE: Thank God. (*Crosses himself in the Catholic manner.*) And may her soul rest in peace.

ROBERT: I only wish she could.

ACHILLE: Don't tell me she's got to stay on the list of enrollees.

ROBERT: Yes and no. Normally I'd love to leave her on the list of lives, but we have a problem.

ACHILLE: We?

ROBERT: (*Pulls out a letter.*) From Corporate, of course. (*Reads out loud.*) "Dear Mr. Robert Vase. Your astonishing increase in Deep South Health Maintenance Organization enrolled lives has come to the attention of headquarters. We congratulate you on the dramatic turnaround. In an effort to emulate your fine example as a best practice model, we are sending Mr. Tournevisse down to get a better understanding of the functioning of your facility. Enclosed is also a bonus check for you and another one for the remarkable Dr. Achille Pierre, internist extraordinaire. Accept them as a token of our appreciation for your remarkable work." (*Extends a check to ACHILLE.*) Want it? You earned it.

ACHILLE: Hell no! I'm not taking a bonus for signing up dead people.

ROBERT: Suit yourself. (*Shrugs his shoulders and pockets both checks.*) Any suggestions?

ACHILLE: When is this guy coming down to do his inspection?

ROBERT: (*Looks at his watch.*) He should be driving in just about now.

ACHILLE: (*Looks around in panic.*) So what have you done to straighten this mess out?

ROBERT: Nothing.

ACHILLE: Nothing! Are you crazy!

ROBERT: No, just depressed.

ACHILLE: (*Comes over and shakes ROBERT by the shoulders.*) Snap out of it! Now! I don't care if you go to prison for the rest of your life, but my sister doesn't deserve it.

ROBERT: So what do you suggest?

ACHILLE: (*Grabs the black book off the desk.*) This is your black book of dead lives, right?

ROBERT: Yes.

ACHILLE: Then dis-enroll them.

ROBERT: When?

ACHILLE: Now!

ROBERT: But I worked so hard putting them all in.

ACHILLE: And now you're going to get rid of them, unless you want to be fired and go to jail for fraud. Your choice.

ROBERT: (*Starts working on his computer. Types as fast as he can. Turns pages of his black book.*) And now?

ACHILLE: Now print out the revised enrollment numbers. (*Yells.*) Now!

(*The printer spits out a bunch of sheets.*)

ROBERT: (*Pulls out the long list of names.*) Ready.

ACHILLE: As ready as we're gong to be.

(*The desk phone rings.*)

ROBERT: Yes, we're expecting him. Please send him in right away.

(*ALEX TOURNEVISSE comes in. He is wearing an expensive suit and carrying a briefcase. ACHILLE and ROBERT rise to meet him.*)

ROBERT: Mr. Tournevisse, what a pleasant surprise. (*Shakes ALEX's hand.*) I'm Robert Vase, hospital administrator, and this is the remarkable Dr. Achille Pierre.

ALEX: (*Shakes hands with ACHILLE.*) Delighted. I have read about your extensive clientele, Dr. Pierre. You must be very busy, indeed. It's really impressive.

ACHILLE: Yes, a truly remarkable clientele. (*Glances at ROBERT and sits down.*)

ALEX: Well, I would like to congratulate you both on your astonishing statistics. We at Corporate have been truly amazed by your increase in enrollment. I've been sent to discover the secret of your success so we could emulate it elsewhere in the system. You are really a shining light, a best practice.

ROBERT: Thank you, thank you. We're so flattered. (*Goes and takes some papers.*) I do have some updated statistics, however, that you will find of some interest. (*Hands the sheets to ALEX.*)

ALEX: (*Examines the sheets with interest. Starts to turn the pages faster and faster.*) These are horrible! You've lost over half of your enrollment in this fiscal quarter. What on earth has happened?

ROBERT: Uh. . . .

ACHILLE: (*Springs up.*) Let me explain, please. (*Goes to the liquor cabinet and serves a couple of drinks.*) Drinks, anyone?

ALEX and ROBERT: No, thank you.

ACHILLE: It's just the usual business cycle, just a bit more dramatic.

ALEX: I'm listening.

ACHILLE: You have your phase of enthusiasm and everything goes up. Everyone is excited and interested. They all want to get on the bandwagon of managed care. Things look wonderful. (*Pauses.*) Then there is the phase of disenchantment.

ALEX: Why?

ACHILLE: Because people start to have other options, other HMOs in larger cities. More providers in other plans. Generally more opportunities. You can't blame them. (*Swings his arms around.*) Here I am, just one country doctor seeing thousands of patients. In Fulton, our nearest urban competitor, they have twenty or thirty doctors to choose from.

They have less waiting times, better customer satisfaction. And *voilà*, a sudden drop in enrollment, it's as natural as night following day.

ALEX: So what's next?

ROBERT: Uh. . . .

ACHILLE: (*Cuts ROBERT off.*) The last phase is the phase of stabilization. Either the plan settles in and reflects its true value to the public or it dies.

ALEX: It dies?

ROBERT: It dies?

ACHILLE: Organizational death, of course. You either stay in the business at some reduced level or you go into oblivion.

ROBERT: Oblivion?

ALEX: Corporate oblivion, I presume.

ACHILLE: Precisely. That fiscal doom starts here and may spread out like an oil slick in an uncontrollable wave of panic.

ROBERT: Panic?

ACHILLE: Yes, panic. Imagine what happens if the events in this lost village get out to Wall Street? (*Pauses.*) Panic! Disenchanted investors. Disappointed hedge fund operators. Of course it could be the end of the ball game, the collapse of the Deep South HMO. The beginning of the end for Corporate.

ALEX: And how can we stop that? What can we do?

ACHILLE: Nothing.

ROBERT and ALEX: Nothing?

ACHILLE: Robert, you sit tight and wait for things to stabilize. . .if they do. (*Speaks to ALEX.*) And you, Alex, you go back with this cautionary tale to Corporate. Let them know how volatile success can be. Explain to them how the phase of enthusiasm leads naturally into the phase of disenchantment, something which can occur with dizzying speed and (*Bends closer to ALEX.*) catastrophic results.

ALEX: (*Clutches his suitcase and stands.*) I think I best be going back to Corporate.

ROBERT: (*Stands to see him go.*) Yes, of course.

ACHILLE: (*Grabs the famous black book off ROBERT's desk.*) And here's a list of people who have just recently left the HMO. You might find it of some interest for your report.

ROBERT: (*Tries to grab the book.*) No, no! That won't be necessary. I'm sure Mr. Tournevisse has enough information as it is.

ALEX: (*Takes the book and flips through it.*) Doucet, Lemoine, Ponthieux, Soileau, Villemarette. (*Stops.*) This reads like the Tunica-Biloxi Parish phone book.

(*ROBERT tries to take the book but ALEX keeps looking at it.*)

ROBERT: Yes, yes, lots of local names. You must be familiar with the area?

ALEX: My great, great uncle on my mother's side lived here many years ago. My grandfather, Adrien Tournevisse used to tell us stories about this place. (*Pauses.*) What was his uncle's name? (*Pauses.*) Charles! Charles Xavier Soileau. (*Flips through the book. Reads.*) Charles Xavier Soileau, born Dec 1, 1922. I think he was born around that time. How odd. Was this patient signed up for the Deep South HMO?

ROBERT: Yes, but dis-enrolled very recently.

ALEX: My great, great uncle died ten year ago or more. That would be years before the Deep South HMO. How strange.

ACHILLE: Soileau's a real common name around here. There must be thousand of them in this parish alone. I've got a couple of hundred in my clientele.

ALEX: Charles Xavier Soileau, born around the same date? That would be a remarkable coincidence indeed? It couldn't be the same man, could it?

ROBERT and ACHILLE: No!

ROBERT: Of course not!

ACHILLE: Just a coincidence. This is a very unique area. Lots of people have the same unusual names.

ALEX: (*Hands the book back to ROBERT.*) Yes, very unique. This does bring back some old memories and some fascinating stories. I think great, great uncle Soileau married a Lemoine, or was it a Dubroc? And there was something about his sister eloping with a Pierre. (*Pauses.*) That's your last name, isn't it? Doctor Achille Pierre?

ACHILLE: Yes.

ALEX: Perhaps we're related? (*Pauses.*) So long ago. They're all dead and gone now I suppose.

ACHILLE: Yes, dead and gone.

ROBERT: Very dead. Very gone. (*Takes the book and stuffs it in his jacket.*)

ALEX: Such a unique area. Don't they say that in Louisiana, even dead people vote?

ROBERT: Twice, but that was generations ago.

ACHILLE: Yes, that's all old history.

ALEX: Well, gentleman, I think I have enough information. If I need anything else, I'll let you both know. (*To ACHILLE.*) Very informative, Doctor. I'm so glad I got to meet you. (*Turns to ROBERT and shakes his hand.*) And very nice to meet you, Mr. Vase. This has been most informative, indeed and Corporate will be fascinated by my findings. (*Exits.*)

ROBERT: (*Slumps down in his chair.*) Do you think he knows?

ACHILLE: (*Shrugs.*) Hard to say. What can we do anyway? The dead are off the books and back in the cemetery. We're still here in the middle of Tunica-Biloxi Parish with our hospital and lots of live patients to take care of.

ROBERT: Thank you, Achille. Thank you for helping out.

ACHILLE: (*Gets two glasses and fills them up. Gives one to ROBERT.*) Here's to all the folks in the black book!

ROBERT: (*Raises his glass.*) To our dead lives! May they rest in peace!

ACHILLE: Amen.

(*ROBERT and ACHILLE touch glasses. Lights dim to dark. Some cheerful Cajun music plays.*)

THE END

MINUET A TROIS
A BLACK COMEDY WITH
CHOREOGRAPHY

CAST OF CHARACTERS

ADBUL EL MALIK (An Al-Qaeda Terrorist). He might be bearded and wears a scarf, perhaps Palestinian one. Besides the beard, he does not have to have any distinguishing characteristics. He can also wear Western attire.

JULIUS COUILLON (Attorney at law). Mr. Couillon should be well-dressed in a suit and tie.

AMERICUS (A beautiful, elegantly dressed lady). She needs to have sparkling tiara, a necklace and one or several bracelets. Her dress may be calf-length or full length, but should appear very elegant, rich, and sophisticated.

SETTING

There are two small cocktail lounge tables, each with a couple of chairs. The tables have LED candle (no fire threats, please.) The tables have white tablecloths.

(ABDUL and JULIUS enter from opposite sides of the stage and greet each other with a friendly hand shake. JULIUS enters from stage right and ABDUL enters from stage left.)

ABDUL: Mr. Couillon, attorney at law. How nice to finally meet you.

JULIUS: And you must be the famous terrorist, Abdul El Malik.

ABDUL: One in the same.

JULIUS: So glad to finally meet you. You have certainly made the headlines with your exploits. Would you like to dance?

ABDUL: But, of course. I would love to learn from the master.

(JULIUS *takes ABDUL's left hand with his right hand and they both turn to face the audience. The music is the Czech folk dance, "Minet," which starts with a slow ¾ time minuet. They both do one waltz step forward and one back, then JULIUS passes ABDUL from the right to the left while changing hands. They repeat the forward and back step and then JULIUS puts ABDUL in front of him. They touch right hand to right hand in the air and walk around each other in four waltzing steps. Then they touch left hands, and then right hands while doing a waltz steps in place. JULIUS finishes turning ABDUL under his raised right arm and pulls ABDUL back to his right side as in the beginning. The music stops and JULIUS and ABDUL take seats at the table stage right. AMERICUS enters and struts around before taking a seat at the table stage left.*)

JULIUS: Wow! Did you see all that jewelry? She's really loaded.

ABDUL: Yes, she's loaded all right. She's loaded with a lot of ill gotten gains, ripped from the world's poor. She's a beauty, she's rich, but she's also a real bitch.

JULIUS: How do you know?

ABDUL: Look at her! Strutting around like she owns the whole world. She thinks she can order everyone around, do whatever she pleases. She's just an overbearing bitch.

JULIUS: With all that money, I guess she must feel powerful. Why not?

ABDUL: She flaunts her wealth and power, consuming the world's resources, supporting all those rich Jews. I tell you, she's a monster.

JULIUS: That's racist. None of that please. After all, I'm part Jewish myself.

ABDUL: Perhaps, but I understand you. You want to take all her money, not destroy her. But that doesn't help me. I want to see her dead. I want her totally annihilated. At least I'm not making any bones about it.

JULIUS: (*Sighs.*) Let me see what I can do. Maybe we can establish a symbiotic relationship. (*Goes over and bows to AMERICUS.*) Julius Couillon, attorney at law, at your service ma'am. May I have the honor of this dance?

AMERICUS: I would be delighted, Mr. Couillon. I really enjoy the thrill of a good dance, especially with such a handsome looking man like you. (*Pauses.*) You look so familiar, Mr. Couillon. Where do I know you?

JULIUS: I've been around. You've probably seen me down at the courthouse, or perhaps on television. I'm often on the news for one thing or another. I just can't seem to stay out of the spotlight.

AMERICUS: How have you been doing lately? You look a little emaciated.

JULIUS: I've really been scraping along. So much competition. These days you can't take a step without stumbling over another lawyer.

AMERICUS: Is there anything I can do to make things better for you?

JULIUS: Oh no, you've really been very accommodating.

AMERICUS: I do try to help everyone out. It's just some people seem to have so much more needs than others. It's hard to satisfy everyone in this day and age: limited resources and unlimited demand. You know what I mean?

JULIUS: Absolutely. Some people would just suck the very life out of you. But for me, a little dance would be just fine for the time being. Madame?

(*JULIUS takes AMERICUS's left hand and leads her to the center of the stage. The Minet plays the second refrain, which is the same as the first. They repeat the figure. Waltz forward, waltz back, AMERICUS passes from right to left. Both waltz forward, waltz and then back, AMERICUS takes two waltz steps and ends facing JULIUS. They touch right hands at shoulder height and waltz around in a circle. When they are back in their original position, they touch left hands to left, right hands to right, while doing a waltz step in place. JULIUS then turns AMERICUS under his right arm and returns her to her original place on his right. He manages to undo her necklace, which he pockets during the dancing. Then JULIUS bows to AMERICUS and escorts her back to her table and JULIUS returns to the table with ABDUL.*)

JULIUS: (*Shows ABDUL the necklace.*) Look what I got. It's worth a fortune. She didn't even notice when I snatched it.

ABDUL: (*Looks with disdain and motions the necklace away.*) I don't want wealth. I want justice.

JULIUS: I thought justice was my line of business.

ABDUL: You must be kidding. Your line if business is settlement, with loads of money going to the lawyers. She is loaded, so I guess we can share in the spoils.

JULIUS: I don't know how we can share. You want to kill her outright and I only want to strip her of her wealth. If she's dead, then I can't get much more out of her, can I?

ABDUL: That's not my problem.

JULIUS: You're tough.

ABDUL: You bet I am. I've been training for this for years. (*Pulls a big knife out of his belt.*) The next dance is mine. The dance of death!

JULIUS: No, no, no. We've got to work together. This woman is my meal ticket and I can't let you kill her, at least not until I've stripped her of everything she's got. Besides, I think I love her.

ABDUL: (*Skeptically.*) Right. Funny kind of love. You steal her blind and you call that love?

(*Both get up and walk over to AMERICUS. They each take a hand. JULIUS is on the left and ABDUL on the right, with AMERICUS in the middle. The music starts the second refrain. JULIUS and ABDUL waltz forward with one waltz step, turn to face AMERICUS on the second waltz step, waltz back to their original places, and turn to face the audience again. AMERICUS waltzes forward on one step, turns on the second and walks back to face her partners on the third and forth. Then they all step toward their own right with the right foot: side, back, side, front, side together. Repeat toward the left: side, back, side, front, side, together. Then AMERICUS hooks right elbows with JULIUS and does two waltz steps and hooks left elbows with ABDUL and does two waltz steps with him, ending up in between them both. During the dancing, JULIUS manages to take off AMERICUS's tiara. ABDUL tries to stab her, but does not succeed. They escort AMERICUS back to her table and ABDUL and JULIUS return to their table.*)

JULIUS: Look at this beauty! (*Shows ABDUL the tiara.*) It's the real thing, too. No doubt about it. I bet this thing is worth a million dollars, maybe more.

ABDUL: (*Very angry.*) You saw me try and stab her. You turned on purpose.

JULIUS: Hey! It's just a dance. Don't get all up tight.

ABDUL: It's not just a dance. It's Jihad. Death to infidels! (*Brandishes the dagger again.*)

JULIUS: Take it easy, Abdul. I can't let you kill her. I told you, she's my meal ticket.

ABDUL: And when you've got everything you want, what then? When she's poor and destitute and depressed, what then? Are you going to send her my way to finish her off?

JULIUS: (*Sighs.*) No. I have to keep her around, if only for old time's sake. (*Plays with the jewelry.*) Besides, you'll get rid of me when you finish with her, so why should I be in a hurry?

ABDUL: (*Plays with his knife.*) Possibly.

JULIUS: And what about all that "people of the book" stuff? What about that? I thought you were supposed to be charitable to the people of the book, Christians and Jews. You have got to show me some mercy whether she's dead or not. I'm half Jewish and I know she's mostly Christian, for what that's worth.

ABDUL: This is war, man. I can not wait until you suck her dry and she dies of exhaustion. We can do it slow and steady, like you, or fast and furiously and be done with it. (*Plays with his knife.*) You will destroy her, too, and perhaps more quickly than me. I can just do a prick here and prick there. She might bleed a little and not die at all. But you suck her to the marrow.

JULIUS: (*Stuffs the jewelry in his pocket.*) Hmmm. Interesting hypothesis.

ABDUL: (*Looks over at AMERICUS and back to JULIUS.*) Go on. There's still the bracelet. What are you waiting for?

JULIUS: (*Gets up and goes over to AMERICUS, who is looking more and more bedraggled.*) Madame, would grant me the honor of this last dance?

AMERICUS: I'm feeling a bit tired. You boys are wearing me out with all of this activity. Can't I sit this one out and catch my breath?

JULIUS: Ah, come on, you look great. You wouldn't disappoint your friends, would you?

AMERICUS: I feel positively exhausted, but I suppose I can dance a little bit more, just to please you.

JULIUS: That's my girl. Give a little more when you think you just can't make it. (*Pulls her up, removing the bracelet in the process.*)

> (*The first reprise begins again for the third and last time. As before, waltz forward, waltz back, pass AMERICUS to the left, waltz forward, waltz back, and she goes in front of JULIUS. Slow circle in four waltz steps, then left to left hand, right to right hand. JULIUS turns AMERICUS under his right arm and returns her to his right side. Meanwhile, ABDUL has gotten up and pulled his dagger. ABDUL approaches the couple. The music becomes quicker and livelier. JULIUS and AMERICUS do one waltz step, then AMERICUS turns under his arm, JULIUS turns under her arm, they waltz backward, then forward and continue with four waltz steps. The sequence starts again. All the while ABDUL is trying to stab AMERICUS. The final four waltz steps end with JULIUS turning AMERICUS under his arm and she falls to the floor, exhausted. JULIUS catches AMERICUS as she falls and holds her in his arms.*)

AMERICUS: That's it, Mr. Couillon, I can't go on anymore. You are exhausting me. My strength just seems to be ebbing away. It's a strange and unfortunate feeling. In fact, I think I'm dying.

ABDUL: (*Stands over them both.*) Good.

JULIUS: Abdul, help me. Call 911. I think she really is dying.

ABDUL: You really expect me to call 911? I'd just as soon give her a final thrust with my dagger. But I doubt that will be necessary. You have done already done my work for me.

JULIUS: Please, speak to me. I'll give you back your jewelry. I'll promise to be good in the future. I'll take care of you. If you die, I will be in mortal danger from the likes of him. (*He points to ABDUL.*)

ABDUL: (*Shakes his head in disgust and throws his dagger at JULIUS.*) Here, if you had any decency, you'll kill yourself, too, and spare me the trouble.

JULIUS: (*Looks down at AMERICUS, who is dead.*) Oh God! She's dead. (*Picks up the knife.*) I can't live without her, not in poverty and misery. What have I done?

ABDUL: You've killed her, you fool. You've sucked out her strength and I don't have to do a thing. If you can't live without her, perhaps you'll just die of unrequited love? (*Laughs demonically and walks off the stage.*)

JULIUS: (*Stands up and looks at AMERICUS's body and at the knife in his hand.*) I really can't live without her, at least not in the manner to which I have grown accustomed. (*Pulls out the jewelry and lets it fall on the stage.*) I'm a dead man anyway. (*Stabs himself and falls to the stage. Lights out.*)

THE END

MRS. DOUGLAS'S CYPRESS TREES

CAST OF CHARACTERS

CORLEY BUCKVIEW: Middle aged man, dressed in a suit and tie, CEO of Red River Hospital.

KRISTINA DUFOUR: Middle aged woman or older, dressed in conservative clothing, employee of the Red River Hospital.

DR. CECIL SOILEAU: Middle aged man in business attire, head of the Quality Health Care Review.

SETTING

The action takes place in Mr. Buckview's office. There is a desk, his chair on one side, and a couple of chairs for visitors on the other side. There can be various papers on the desk, plus a lamp and other paraphernalia of an office, included a manila envelope with a photo inside.

DUFOUR: You cannot cut down those trees, Mr. Buckview!

BUCKVIEW: Mrs. Dufour, we have gone over this issue already with the architects. There is no reasonable way to save those trees if we are going to complete the hospital expansion plans.

DUFOUR: I can't believe that. I can't believe your talented architects can't design an atrium or put an indentation in the side of the new building. For heaven's sake, if we can put people on the moon and invent the internet, then we can save two cypress trees.

BUCKVIEW: Mrs. Dufour. . . .

DUFOUR: Please call me Kristina.

BUCKVIEW: Kristina, you work in the lab here in the hospital, don't you?

DUFOUR: Yes, I do. I supervise the hematology section. I've been there for twenty years.

BUCKVIEW: That's very nice. I appreciate loyalty. I also understand and applaud your interest in the environment. But these two trees are only a couple of swamp cypress trees like a million others around this place.

DUFOUR: Only two swamp cypress! How can you say that?

BUCKVIEW: Please, call me Corley.

DUFOUR: Corley, those are not just two cypress trees. Those are Mrs. Mary Douglas's cypress trees.

BUCKVIEW: Am I supposed to know Mrs. Douglas?

DUFOUR: No, of course not, she's dead. She's been dead for seven years already.

BUCKVIEW: You're worried about some dead lady's trees?

DUFOUR: This is not just some dead lady. She was a wonderful woman who touched many lives with her kindness. Apparently you were unaware that she lived in the little house on a property where those two trees are located. Her family lived there. Her father was Italian, a shoemaker, I think. I grew up in another little house located across the bayou. Mary Santorini, that was her maiden name, played with me for hours under the shade of those two trees. They were already there when the house was built at the turn of the century. It was just a little place, but Luigi, Mary's father, loved that house and he loved those two old trees. He said they protected the house and his family and brought him luck.

BUCKVIEW: That's very touching, but the hospital has owned that property for years. They built a parking lot at least fifty years ago.

DUFOUR: That's right. Mr. Santorini sold the property to the hospital with the understanding that the house would be demolished, but that the trees would remain standing. And they did. The parking lot was built around them.

BUCKVIEW: Good grief! That was a half a century ago. Times have changed, needs change. We're closing the whole street for this hospital expansion. It means jobs for this area, more money for this area. We can't sacrifice progress for a couple of trees.

DUFOUR: But I promised Mary. I promised her to look after those trees. She died with Alzheimer's disease. She couldn't remember what she ate for breakfast, but she would still grab my arm and look into my eyes. Somewhere, deep down inside, she remembered those two trees and she would ask me "How are my trees doing, Kristy?" She always called me Kristy. "How are my cypress trees doing?" Each time, until she really couldn't talk anymore, she asked about her trees. Now she's gone. There's no one left but me to look after them. There's no one else who cares.

BUCKVIEW: I'm afraid you're mistaking on that point. I've gotten a half a dozen letters here since some crackpot mailed a picture of those two trees into the paper and those fools published it.

DUFOUR: Really?

BUCKVIEW: (*Takes some letter from his desk and begins to read.*) "Dear Mr. Buckview, I grew up downtown and I always drove by those two great trees on my way to work. They always seemed to be standing guard for the hospital, etc., etc." Or this one, "Dear Mr. Buckview, Can't we live in peace with the environment? I can't bear to see one more historic tree sacrificed in the name of progress. Etc., etc." Or maybe this one, "Dear Mr. Buckview, Every murdered tree is one more soldier lost in our war against global warming, etc., etc." (*Drops the letters on his desk.*) Mrs.

Dufour, Kristina, I have a fiduciary responsibility to the shareholders of this hospital. I cannot justify unreasonable expenses to save two cypress trees, regardless of their sentimental value. These are not endangered species. These are not historically significant trees. These are two swamp cypress trees standing next to a downtown road that is also going to be sacrificed in the name of progress. The city has approved the plan. I'm afraid I can't help you.

DUFOUR: Then I'll chain myself to one of the trees and keep them from being chopped down. No one is going to allow you to brutalize a helpless old lady trying to save a tree.

BUCKVIEW: Helpless? I hardly consider you as helpless. But on a practical level, there are two very serious flaws in your goofy scheme. The first is that you happen to be a hospital employee and I have every right to fire any employee who brings negative publicity to this hospital.

DUFOUR: Are you threatening me?

BUCKVIEW: You bet I am.

DUFOUR: And what about my constitutional right to free speech?

BUCKVIEW: I repeat, we have the absolute right to fire any employee who brings negative publicity to this hospital, regardless of their motivations or justification. This is private property, not public property and those trees are located on hospital grounds. (*Pauses.*) But the second flaw in your argument is even more serious. (*Pauses again and points out the window.*) The trees have already been cut down.

DUFOUR: (*Rushes to an imaginary window and looks out.*) My God! They're gone. I came in the back way because the road was closed. I didn't even see that they were gone. What have you done?

BUCKVIEW: We had them chopped down last night as a precaution against any unnecessary disturbances.

151

DUFOUR: You murdered those trees. You're a heartless monster!

BUCKVIEW: No, I'm the CEO of a multimillion dollar hospital and I can not be sabotaged by sentimentalists and tree hugging crackpots.

DUFOUR: (*Shakes her head.*) I can't believe it. They're gone. Just like that. In one night. Two hundred years old and gone in one night.

BUCKVIEW: Yes, they're gone. But you are still here, Kristina Dufour, and you still have a job. That's something, isn't it? (*Hands her an envelope.*) I even have a gift for you.

DUFOUR: (*Opens the envelope.*) It's a photograph of Mary's trees. (*Hands it back to him.*) Thank you, but I have my own document. (*Pulls an envelope out of her purse.*) And this one is for you.

BUCKVIEW: It's a letter of resignation.

DUFOUR: Yes. I'm resigning. (*Fishes in her purse and pulls out another document and reads.*) I also have this. "I undersigned Luigi Santorini agree to sell my home and property to the board of Red River Hospital with the understanding that present and futures owners will not remove the two cypress trees from above mentioned property. Signed and notarized." (*Hands the paper to Mr. Buckview.*)

BUCKVIEW: (*Examines the paper.*) It looks authentic. But it's a worthless piece of paper.

DUFOUR: It's a signed contract, Mr. CEO. And even if it's not legal, at least it was a moral obligation. You've committed a breach of contract.

BUCKVIEW: (*Throws the paper back at Kristina.*) It's a worthless piece of paper. (*Picks up her letter of resignation.*) But your letter of resignation is not. I accept your resignation, effective immediately. You will clear out of your office today and I will have hospital security supervise your departure. You have caused enough of a headache already.

DUFOUR: Do what you must. (*Points out the window.*) But your future building is cursed. It is cursed before it rises from the ground. The roots of Mary's trees will scream out silent cries that will rise through the girders and into the walls and ceiling. Nothing good will come of it. (*Pauses.*) You think you have won, but the trees have won. They will have their justice if it takes ten or twenty or a hundred years. Luigi and Mary and the trees will have justice as God is my witness.

BUCKVIEW: Are you quite finished with your hysterical theatrics? This is madness. (*Presses on his intercom.*) Mrs. Smith, please send in the security guards to remove Mrs. Dufour immediately.

DUFOUR: Don't bother. I'll leave on my own. (*Strides off.*)

BUCKVIEW: (*Picks up the photo of the trees and looks at them a minute and then he tears up the photo and throws it into the garbage can.*) Damn trees!

> (*BUCKVIEW sits down at his desk. No sooner does he sit down, then there is a knock on the door and DR. SOILEAU enters. BUCKVIEW stands up again.*)

BUCKVIEW: Can I help you?

SOILEAU: I'm Dr. Soileau, here for my two-thirty appointment.

BUCKVIEW: Soileau? (*Leafs through his agenda.*)

SOILEAU: I'm from the Quality Health Care Review.

BUCKVIEW: Oh, that Dr. Soileau.

SOILEAU: I'm medical director of the QHCR. We made a site visit last spring, remember?

BUCKVIEW: Of course, of course. Please sit down.

SOILEAU: (*Takes some papers from his briefcase and hands them to BUCKVIEW, then takes a copy for himself.*) This is your report card. We talked about it last spring and now we have adequate statistics to make an official report. We have been giving them to each of the various hospital CEOs around the state prior to publishing them officially on the web.

BUCKVIEW: (*Flips through the sheets.*) Well, how'd we do? Everyone knows that Red River Hospital is the best in the area. It's general knowledge.

SOILEAU: Sometimes perception is more important than reality, but in this case, I'm afraid there is some room for improvement.

BUCKVIEW: What do you mean?

SOILEAU: If you turn to page twelve, you'll see your composite score for quality indicators. It's above the state average, but below the national average.

BUCKVIEW: That's good, isn't it?

SOILEAU: Yes. It's better than the state average, but less than your cross town competitor's average. They have been devoting considerable resources to identifying and improving quality indicators. As you can see, they have been scoring above state and national averages in every category.

BUCKVIEW: This is interesting. I'll be sure and share this with our medical staff. They will certainly be fascinated.

SOILEAU: I assume they are already well aware of our program.

BUCKVIEW: Some of our thought leaders are already aware.

SOILEAU: And not the general staff?

BUCKVIEW: Yes, of course they are. But they can also be a bit recalcitrant at times. There are a lot of changes going on now: a new computer system, the hospitalist program, and the intensivists. Sometimes it's a bit much for any of them to assimilate. Also, some of the physicians resent what they perceive as cookbook medicine being imposed on them from the outside.

SOILEAU: (*Stands up and begins to pace in front of the BUCKVIEW's desk.*) Let me be frank with you. This is not just an academic question. These quality indicators, whatever you or your medical staff may think of them, are evidence-based medicine. This report card will become general knowledge soon, not only to your competitors, but to every insurance company in the state and the nation.

BUCKVIEW: And I'm sure our competitor will make the most of it, too.

SOILEAU: And well they should. But it's not just a question of competition. You are aware of the pay-for-performance initiatives.

BUCKVIEW: Yes, I'm aware of the theory.

SOILEAU: (*Stops pacing and stands directly in front of BUCKVIEW.*) It's not just a theory. Medicare is interested in quality. This state has the highest national costs and the lowest health indicators in the nation. It's intolerable and the federal government will not put up with it any longer. (*Sits down and flips through the papers and shows BUCKVIEW one of them*). Every hospital falling below the national, not the state, average will receive less reimbursement.

BUCKVIEW: You're kidding.

SOILEAU: Do I look like I'm kidding?

BUCKVIEW: That could cost us millions in Medicare reimbursements.

SOILEAU: (*Flips through the pages.*) One million, five hundred and seventy thousand, to be precise.

BUCKVIEW: A million and a half?

SOILEAU: Yes. It starts this year if you don't manage to improve your statistics immediately.

BUCKVIEW: We'll have to hire extra people just to start compiling the data and insuring compliance.

SOILEAU: Yes. That's something we talked about last spring. (*Stands up and walks to the window and looks out.*) Beautiful day out there.

BUCKVIEW: How am I supposed to do this with a medical staff that thinks all these projects are a Socialist plot to rob them of their therapeutic liberties? (*Stands up.*) I can't even get them to fill out the forms, much less follow the recommendations. It's crazy.

SOILEAU: (*Still looks out the window.*) No, it's not crazy, it's necessary to restore solvency to Medicare. (*Spins around to face BUCKVIEW.*) And if your medical staff stops trying to fight the Civil War all over again, then maybe you can make some progress. (*Looks back out the window.*) Some construction going on over there?

BUCKVIEW: Yes. Expansion of the emergency room and more acute care beds.

SOILEAU: Business must be booming.

BUCKVIEW: We're doing well enough. But Corporate's never satisfied. You know how that is.

SOILEAU: So I guess Corporate is not going to be happy about an avoidable 1.5 million dollar loss in reimbursements, is it?

BUCKVIEW: No.

SOILEAU: Sometimes a modest investment will yield the best dividends. So I suggest you allocate the necessary resources to improving your quality report card and avoid the unpleasant financial consequences.

BUCKVIEW: Of course.

SOILEAU: By the way, weren't there two magnificent cypress tress over there, just on the other side of the road?

BUCKVIEW: (*Shakes his head and slumps down in his chair.*) Yes.

SOILEAU: What happened to them?

BUCKVIEW: We chopped them down to make room for the expansion.

SOILEAU: (*Shakes his head.*) What a pity. They were beautiful trees. I noticed them last spring. (*Returns to his chair and picks up his briefcase.*) I'm somewhat of a tree hugger myself.

BUCKVIEW: Yes. I loved those trees, too. We really debated on cutting them down. In fact, I have a lovely photo of them somewhere here. (*Looks around his desk and then down into the garbage can.*) Or at least I thought I did.

SOILEAU: If you every come across it, let me know. I'm also a bit of an amateur artist and I thought of painting a picture of those beauties. You'll let me know if you find the photo, won't you.

BUCKVIEW: Sure. No problem.

SOILEAU: Well, I need to be going. Do you have any questions?

(*SOILEAU AND BUCKVIEW stand and shake hands.*)

BUCKVIEW: No. I believe I got the message.

SOILEAU: I hope so. It would be a pity to sacrifice two lovely trees to build a new building only to fill it with substandard medical practices, wouldn't you agree?

BUCKVIEW: Yes. Of course.

(SOILEAU leaves the room. BUCKVIEW sits back in his chair. He bends over and begins to retrieve pieces of the photo and puts them on his desk. He unsuccessfully tries to put them back together like a puzzle. With an angry gesture, BUCKVIEW wipes the pieces off the desk and they flutter to the floor.)

BUCKVIEW: Damn Dufour! Damn Soileau! Damn trees! How many cypresses will I have to plant to get out from this curse? (*Grabs his Rolodex or phone director and begins flipping through it frantically.*) Where the hell is Dufour's phone number? (*Punches in the number on his cell phone.*) Hello. Kristina, this is Mr. Buckview. (*Pauses.*) Please don't hang up. I really need to talk to you. (*Pauses.*) Yes, I was wrong. I was very wrong to cut down those trees. And that's what I need to talk to you about. I would like to plant some more trees to replace them. (*Pauses.*) I don't know how many. Ten? Twenty? (*Pauses.*) A hundred! You want me to plant 100 new tress just to replace two lousy swamp cypresses? (*Pauses.*) No! No! Don't hang up. One hundred trees would be just fine. Also, I need to hire you back for this tree-planting project and something else, something to do with quality indicators. I think that with your sense of social consciousness and organization, you will be just the woman we need for the job. (*Pauses.*) That would be fine. Just come around tomorrow afternoon. And could you do me one small favor? (*Pauses.*) No. Nothing shifty. I would just like you to bring me a copy of your photo of Mrs. Douglas's cypress trees. There's a friend of mine in Baton Rouge who would appreciate it. (*Pauses.*) Thank you so much. And see you tomorrow. (*Shuts off his phone and sits down at his desk. He puts his hands on his head and shakes it back and forth.*) Damn trees!

(Lights dim to dark.)

THE END

NEPUJDU Z HOSPODY
(I WON'T LEAVE THE PUB)

CAST OF CHARACTERS

JARMILLA KOSTEL: late 40's, early 50's. She may be a little overweight and has a slight Southern regional accent.

KARL KOSTEL: 50's. He also has a country accent, without any Czech resonance.

SETTING

Home of Jarmilla and Karl Kostel in Libuse, Louisiana. The set contains a table and a couple of simple chairs, which are offset a little, leaving the larger part of the stage for dancing. On the table is a little portable CD player.

(The lights come up with JARMILLA and KARL holding each other's hands up in the air with the left hands over the right. He is trying to turn her around to create a window, but they are hopelessly entangled. JARMILLA is tripping over KARL's feet and falling.)

JARMILLA: No! No! No! Not like that Karl. You have to let me turn under your arms.

KARL: *(Drops JARMILLA's hands in frustration.)* For God's sake, Jarmilla. It's a hard figure to get right.

JARMILLA: I know, dear. But it will look great when we finally get the hang of it. Now take my right hand with your right hand. And take my left hand with your left hand over the right. Lift up your arms. And let me twist under you.

(KARL tries again. They get a little further along in the dance, then get tangled up and stop.)

KARL: I can't do this! Can we stop and take a little break at least? You're killing me with this thing.

JARMILLA: Okay. Let's take a little break. I'll get a couple of beers. Is that all right?

(KARL nods and JARMILLA goes off stage and reappears with a couple of Pilsen beers. JARMILLA hands one to KARL and they both sit down and take a swig.)

KARL: Thanks. I needed this.

JARMILLA: The beer's good, isn't it?

KARL: Yeah. A lot better than our dancing. *(Drinks again.)* Honey, do you really want to keep doing this Czech dancing?

JARMILLA: You mean today?

KARL: No. I mean at all. Do you really want to keep folk dancing at all?

JARMILLA: Keep dancing! What a silly question. Of course I want to keep dancing. I like to dance. When I get dressed up in my costume, I feel special, pretty. I know I'm not that beautiful, but in that gorgeous costume, I feel beautiful. Besides, it's our heritage, our culture.

KARL: I guess. But I just can't seem to get the hang of these complicated dances.

JARMILLA: These dances come straight from the Old World, straight from Central Europe to Central Louisiana. They're our precious heritage.

KARL: *(Takes another sip of beer and looks at the bottle.)* Pilsen beer. Now this is part of our precious heritage that I can appreciate. As for the rest, neither of us speaks Czech. Only a few old people around here still do. And all this dancing and costume stuff, it's just a charade. It's all made up, Jarmilla.

JARMILLA: It is not! Our costumes come from Bohemia and Moravia. We copied them from originals right from there.

KARL: Yeah, originals that the Parkers brought back from one of their trips. It's just copying, like Disney World, a fake Bohemian village right here in Central Louisiana. Sure, it's really pretty, but it's just make-believe.

JARMILLA: But the dances are real dances from over there and you know it.

KARL: Yeah, also brought back from the Old World by the Parkers. Hell, the only dances our parents still did around here were waltzes and polkas, not all these fancy folk dances the Parkers taught us.

JARMILLA: Karl, I am not going to talk about the Parkers. Besides, if you don't want to learn about your culture for your sake, or mine, what about for your son, Peter.

KARL: Peter? What does he care? He just comes along and does what we're doing. Do you think he really cares about any of this folklore stuff? Dances? Costumes?

JARMILLA: Yes, I do. I think it gives him a very important sense of place, a cultural identity.

KARL: Well, maybe you are right about that, but does it give him a job? He needs employment. He needs a well paying job and a place of his own. That's what he needs, not imported folk dances and fake ethnic costumes.

JARMILLA: You can me so mean. Peter's been trying to get a job for months. There's just nothing out there. And he's taking classes, too.

KARL: So we just keep paying the bills and he learns how to do Czech folk dancing for the good of his cultural self esteem. That's a wonderful arrangement. Besides, there are jobs out there. He just might not feel qualified.

JARMILLA: That's not true. He has applied everywhere and just hasn't gotten accepted. Like at the paper mill.

KARL: He never applied to the paper mill. I talked to Frank Beaumont out there. Peter never showed up when they called for applicants.

JARMILLA: But he told me he just didn't get accepted.

KARL: He didn't apply. Believe me or not. He just never went out there to apply.

JARMILLA: But why?

KARL: Ask him. Maybe he was too tired from at that folk dancing?

JARMILLA: *(Rises up.)* Enough chatter. I think we need to get back to practice. We are never going to be ready for the Czech Festival at this rate. You need this practice. You've missed enough rehearsals as it is.

KARL: I happen to have been working, honey. I can't just drop everything at a construction site and tell my boss I've got to stop pouring cement and leave for folk dancing.

> *(KARL drags himself up. They get back into their position with the left hands over the right. KARL lifts up his arms and JARMILLA twists under. They form the window and began to turn and then untwist as they get tangled.)*

KARL: Oh hell! Forget this shit. I'm sick of it.

JARMILLA: Don't dare you give up like that, Karl Kostel!

KARL: *(Plops down and resumes his beer.)* I am giving up. I'm sick of this dance. In fact, I'm sick of all this folklore crap. I'm sick of my work buddies calling me a fairy because of my feathered hat and braided vest. *(Imitates another man mocking him)* Oh, Karl. You look so sweet in that cute little hat. And you turn and twist like a real ballerina. *(Reverts to his regular voice.)* Do you think I like to hear that bullshit over and over again? For what? For folklore? For my Czech heritage? I've been playing along with this for years. Now give me a break and let me throw in the towel. It's your thing, not mine. It's the Parker's thing, not mine. Go ahead and dance with Peter if you want to and if you don't mind dancing with your own son. *(Finishes off the beer and slams down the bottle.)* I'm done with all this crap. I'm giving up.

JARMILLA: *(Sits down and studies KARL.)* What kind of a message do you think that sends to your son?

KARL: That I don't like to get dressed up like a clown and dance around like a fairy. That I don't like my friends and coworkers and even members of my own family making fun of me. That I'd rather be out hunting or fishing. How about that message? Is it really such a bad message to convey to our son?

JARMILLA: That's not a bad message. But I don't think it's the message you are sending him.

KARL: Then what message do you think I'm sending?

JARMILLA: I think you're sending him the message that if something is hard, or different, or if people make fun of you, then you give up.

KARL: That's crap and you know it! Whether I learn a folk dance or not doesn't mean a rat's ass to Peter.

JARMILLA: Maybe. Maybe not. But do you want him to throw in the towel when things get a little tough? Do you want him to give up when other people criticize him or make fun of him? Do you want him to say he's applying for jobs and then not go at all?

KARL: You're exaggerating and you know it.

JARMILLA: Maybe. But just think about it. Was there any time your dad just gave up on something.

KARL: Of course not. He worked like dog. He worked through poverty. He put up with all those town people calling him a Bohunk. He picked potatoes until his hands bled. That man worked and worked and he never gave up. After that hurricane blew through here, he helped rebuild that Czech hall and never asked for a penny for his time or his lumber. That man was a saint and don't you dare say anything bad about him.

JARMILLA: I'm not saying anything bad. I'm just pointing out that your son is going to look at you in the same way. And he's going to expect the same behavior.

KARL: For heaven's sake. How can you compare some silly dancing with struggling through the depression and putting up with hateful local snobs?

JARMILLA: They're both lessons in life, aren't they. Preserving culture. Passing it on to your children.

KARL: Don't be nuts. I'm getting up every morning and going to work and then working around here on the weekends. I'm helping Uncle Fred with his damn potatoes and Uncle Harvey with his lumber. My hands, my knees, my back all hurt from all that forced labor. But there is a roof over our head and food on the table. Isn't that the work ethic that needs to be passed on? Not this fake culture crap. (*Pauses.*) Dad went to the dances. He knew how to waltz and polka. But he never even heard of all these fancy steps. He never put on a weird hats and embroidered vests. That guy never got out of his overalls. He did speak Czech, though, and that's more than I can say for us.

JARMILLA: That's all true. And he was a good man, a great man. But he would be proud of you in your weird hat and pretty vest. He would burst with pride to see you twirling around and teaching your son to do the same. And don't say you can't speak Czech.

KARL: Come on! Saying *pivo* and *kolache* doesn't count.

JARMILLA: Why not? And maybe this dancing thing is easier than learning Czech. Your dad just didn't have the chance to learn. I think he would have liked it. And, as you said, he never gave up on anything and you shouldn't either.

KARL: *(Swigs on the empty bottle.)* Yeah, he was almost a saint. But he did give up on something.

JARMILLA: What?

KARL: When he finished high school, he talked about going to college, to forestry school. But he gave up on the idea to stay and work on the farm.

JARMILLA: That wasn't his fault. That was the depression. It was a horrible time. Nobody had the money to go to college. Everyone had to work just to eat.

KARL: That's true. But when I finished high school, I talked to him about going away to school, maybe in engineering. I was always pretty good at math. And he just listened. He never said anything.

JARMILLA: But that was your choice not to go to college, not his.

KARL: I know, but with just a little push, a little encouragement. I think I would have given it a try. And who knows where we would be now or how we would be living? *(Pauses.)* I just needed a little push. I think I could have gotten a scholarship, worked in the summers. Now look at me, I'm just a manual laborer, I pour concrete all day. Look at my hands, rough and scaly, covered with calluses.

JARMILLA: *(Moves across and takes KARL's hands.)* Your hands are beautiful. They were the first thing I noticed when I met you.

KARL: Not my handsome face?

JARMILLA: No. Not your handsome face. Your strong hands. I liked their look and I liked their feel. And I still do. They're a real man's hands. *(Puts them on her face.)* If you don't want to keep dancing, that's all right. You don't have to. And Peter may or may not want to continue if you don't. But he'll still admire you whether you dance or not. I know he will. And I will, too. Besides, I can always dance with your cousin, Harry. He's a good dancer, with a good memory for dance, and very strong hands, too.

KARL: Strong hands! Sure, strong enough to beat up his first and second wives. That's pretty strong.

JARMILLA: But he loves to dance. He gets me in his grip and just spins me around like a top. It's a little intoxicating, you know, like a strong drink after a hot day's work. He may not be such a nice person, but he's a very good dancer. And not bad looking either. Don't you agree?

KARL: *(Sighs and frowns.)* Okay. Let's leave Harry out of this. I'm willing to give this dance another chance. For Peter's sake, of course. So, can we just try the turning part?

JARMILLA: Left hands over right. Lift up your arms.

> *(JARMILLA turns under and they make the window. As they circle around, they are looking at each other with great intensity. KARL untwists her.)*

JARMILLA: Now I turn while I'm going backwards as your do your boot slapping step.

> *(KARL claps his hands, then slaps his upraised right foot, then repeats with the left foot. Then KARL does three quick right-left-right claps on his thighs and slaps his upraised right foot. KARL repeats the slap with his upraised left foot.)*

KARL: Good God. I think I got it right.

JARMILLA: It was just right, Karl! It was perfect! Are you ready to try it with music?

KARL: Do you think we're ready?

JARMILLA: Not quite. We need to get in the right mind set. Now, look at me and imagine me wearing my white blouse with the ruffled sleeves and my red and green embroidered vest.

KARL: The one with your boobs pressing out?

JARMILLA: Yes, that's the one, but please leave the boob part out of it. Now imagine my white skirt, all billowing out, and my blue, print apron and black, shiny boots. Do you have that mental image?

KARL: I've got it all.

JARMILLA: Now imagine yourself standing tall with that gorgeous black hat all decorated with feathers and beads, and your red vest with the blue trim that I sewed on stitch by stitch. And your shirt with the embroidery that Aunt Helen sewed for you.

KARL: The one I spilled ketchup on at the last Czech Festival.

JARMILLA: Yes, that one, but without the ketchup part. Well, how do we look?

KARL: I don't know about me, but you look just beautiful.

JARMILLA: Cheap and fake?

KARL: No. You look like the real thing, a Czech princess. You look like Princess Libuse herself. *(Kisses her.)* My beautiful, Czech princess. Now can we get started?

JARMILLA: *(Laughs and kisses KARL's hands.)* My handsome Czech prince with his strong hands. *(Goes over and starts the little CD player.)* Let's go.

> *(The music is the Czech dance "Nepujdu z Hospody" (*I Won't leave the Pub*). The choreography is that of Eva and Radek Rejskovi. The dance is 1 minute 43 seconds long, but only half or less needs to be used with the steps from the second part of the dance. That portion contains the window movement and the boot slapping. The volume should be fairly loud. The couple dances without error and the lights dim to dark as KARL ends with the final boot slap.)*

THE END

PEACE WITH HONOR

CAST OF CHARACTERS

SALLY: George's wife.

GEORGE: Sally's husband.

SETTING

The stage is empty except for a kitchen table, a couple of chairs, a newspaper, a pot of coffee and a couple of cups. Although some actions are indicated, there can be a lot of moving around and gesticulating up to the director's discretion. It need not be a static scene.

(SALLY is sitting at a small table. She is reading a newspaper and drinking a cup of coffee. There are two chairs. GEORGE comes in with another cup of coffee and a pot of coffee which he sets on a trivet. He goes to SALLY, who lowers her newspaper, and gives GEORGE gives SALLY a kiss. The couple can be going through the motions of getting dressed and ready for work.)

GEORGE: *(Sits down and begins to drink his coffee.)* Anything new in the world?

SALLY: Another bombing over there. Another ten American soldiers dead. Plus thirty innocent civilians, of course.

GEORGE: Did they release the names of the soldiers who got killed?

SALLY: Not yet. They're waiting until the next of kin are notified, as usual.

GEORGE: God, I hope Michael's not one of them. Gloria and Carl must be sick with worry every time they pick up a paper or listen to the news. What torture this has to be for them.

SALLY: Your sister and brother-in-law are great people with a great outlook. They know Michael is there because he wants to be and they are willing to accept whatever happens.

GEORGE: I don't think we should be over there at all. Those people hate us and we're never gong to change them no matter how long we stay and how many people are killed.

SALLY: *(Lowers her paper to look at GEORGE.)* Now aren't we little mister anti-war radical this morning. You sound like one of those liberal Hollywood types. Michael's over there and I'm proud of him, just like his parents are. And if we had a son, I'd be proud of him if he were there, too.

GEORGE: Well, we don't have a son to send over there, thank God. And perhaps those Hollywood liberals are right. Perhaps we should have never sent our troops over there. It's just turning into a quagmire and Michael is right in the middle of it.

SALLY: So you think we should have just stayed out of that place and let that country go completely rotten?

GEORGE: Yes, let them just stay as bad as they have always been. People have been fighting in that part of the world for centuries. One group against another, one country against another. Does it really matter to us? Do you really think they pose any real threat to the United States? Do you really think that Michael being over there will make any kind of difference at all?

SALLY: Of course Michael will make a difference. And as far as threats go, of course they're a threat. If that country goes to the enemy, the whole area will goes down the drain. It will get worse and worse, more and more hostile. Yes, I think they're a threat, a real threat to us, to liberty, to democracy, and to all of Western civilization. And Michael's doing his part to contribute to that defense. To your defense, I might add, Mr. Liberal.

GEORGE: Oh, don't get carried away Mrs. Patriotic Zealot. *(Sips on his coffee.)* I don't believe we are in any danger. And besides, if that place is such a threat to us, why doesn't the rest of the world agree?

SALLY: We do have allies, lots of them. Our friends from countries all over the world agree with us and have sent troops to back us up.

GEORGE: Yeah, right. So why are all the so-called Allied casualties American?

SALLY: That's not true and you know it.

GEORGE: Okay. Why are ninety percent of the so-called allied casualties American?

SALLY: And the local troops? What about them? A lot more of them are dying everyday than our boys.

GEORGE: The locals who fight with us are considered traitors by most people in their own country and many outside of it. Besides, a lot of our true, traditional allies have already expressed their disapproval of this war and are not offering any help at all, just criticism. What does that suggest?

SALLY: Traditional allies? How dare you talk about allies! Those people are just ungrateful bastards. Look at what we did for them in World War II. Now they turn around and treat us like international war criminals. And those insufferable French hypocrites! My God, they don't appreciate a thing we ever did for them. I can't stand those people. We bailed them out twice and they still stab us in the back.

GEORGE: This is French Roast, dear. Would you like another cup? *(Holds up the coffee pot.)*

SALLY: *(Pushes her coffee cup away.)* If it's French, then I've had enough!

GEORGE: *(Laughs and pours SALLY some more.)* Don't be ridiculous. Let me warm up that cup. Perhaps the rest of the world knows something we don't? Maybe if that godforsaken country we're fighting in just goes ahead and does its own thing. I don't think it would make a bit of difference to us, despite what some of our leaders want us to believe.

SALLY: Michael believed them, or he wouldn't have gone. I'm sure he felt he was doing something for America and for the people over there. He wants to make this sorry world a better place to live in for himself and for the rest of us. He might not be an intellectual, but he has a real intuitive sense of his broader purpose in what you want us to believe is only a regional conflict. What about that?

GEORGE: That's ridiculous! Michael didn't believe in all that sort of thing. He wanted to get the GI bill so he could go to college. Besides, I don't think he even knew the name of the country he was going to fight in.

SALLY: That's insulting. Michael may not have been the valedictorian, but he's not an idiot either. I think he believes in what he's doing and he certainly knew where he was going. And what right do you or any of us have to take his patriotic motivation away? The boy's finally growing up. He's doing something noble, something for the good of the nation. Your sister and brother-in-law are proud of him and we should be, too. Don't take their pride away. It's not fair to Michael or Gloria or Carl. Besides, we don't have any sons to give to the cause of the defense of liberty.

GEORGE: Oh, and that's my fault, too. Not only don't I believe all that official propaganda, but I couldn't even make a son to donate to the cause. *(Pauses.)* That's plain mean spirited and you know it.

SALLY: I'm sorry. I didn't mean it that way.

(SALLY goes over and tries to embrace GEORGE, but he pushes her away.)

GEORGE: Come on. I'm not exactly in the mood, and especially with someone who's gullible enough to believe all that rubbish coming out of Washington. Certainly you don't believe all that crap?

SALLY: Yes, I do. And so do a lot of intelligent people, including our president.

GEORGE: Michael's young and naive, so he has an excuse. But our president, with all due respect, is a fool.

SALLY: He is not a fool.

GEORGE: Yes, he is!

SALLY: No, he's not!

(GEORGE AND SALLY sulk a little in silence.)

GEORGE: I will admit that the president has some clever advisors. But they are just out for their own personal agendas, whatever they might be. They want kids like Michael to get sucked into this mess for their own selfish ends. They probably all own stock in defense industries.

SALLY: So you believe this is some sort of high level right wing government conspiracy?

GEORGE: Maybe not. But I do think there are people in Washington who are more concerned about making money and keeping their political power than doing what is good for the rest of us.

SALLY: That's pretty cynical. Now you're really turning into a cynical, radical, Hollywood type.

GEORGE: Thanks for the compliment. *(Pauses for a few seconds.)* I can't help think about Gloria and Carl and all the other parents of American boys. Each soldier killed is someone's child. Remember when Michael played in our yard with toy guns. Remember when he fell out of the tree and tore open his knee while we were baby-sitting for him? Remember how he cried and we comforted him, then sat in the emergency room and waited, just as if we were his own parents? Those daily lists of casualties in the newspaper are not just numbers, they're real people like Michael. And don't forget all the civilian children caught in the crossfire. Could you live with yourself if you contributed to the death of someone's little boy?

SALLY: Those are the very children Michael's fighting for. Don't you understand? He is over there fighting so that those little children and babies can group up to be free and productive citizens in a peaceful, democratic country at peace with its neighbors and. . . .

GEROGE: And an ally of the United States of America. Don't forget that.

SALLY: And why not?

GEORGE: Because it's not worth it. You know what they say about history. Those who fail to study the past are doomed to repeat it. Remember Bismarck? He told the German parliament that all the Balkans were not worth the life of one German soldier. So how can you tell me that the miserable country where our poor soldiers are dying is worth it to us? They're not a real threat, despite what misinformation we might be getting. All we've done by being over there is to mobilize our real enemies there and around the world and create a vicious on-going civil war. All that because of our misguided foreign policy decisions. I just can't stand thinking about dead young men, children, and their grieving families here and there. I can't stand to think that Gloria and Carl could lose their only son and we could lose our only nephew for that stupid, pointless war. I just can't stand it anymore.

SALLY: (*Goes over and tries to comfort GEROGE.*) I know it upsets you, but sometimes we just have to trust our leaders. Besides, I don't think we should send our enemies the message that the American public is divided about this war. That will only encourage them to prolong the conflict. We must stand united. We must support Michael and all the other troops. When Michael leaves that godforsaken place, he must leave in peace and with honor. There's no other way to do it.

GEORGE: Peace with honor, eh? And when will that be? How many more will have to die before we reach that point? Will Michael have to die? Will he have to come home in a black body bag?

SALLY: That's morbid!

GEORGE: I love Michael. I support Michael. I support every one of those poor boys sent to that hell hole just like Michael. But I do not support the president or his administration for sending them there to die.

SALLY: I'm sure you love Michael, too. But if you do, why would you want to be accused of being so lovingly unpatriotic?

GEORGE: I will not be treated as unpatriotic for opposing our participation there. What good is peace with honor for those who are dead? If Michael's killed, will he be able to hear it when those old farts in Washington finally decide that they're making a mistake and need to rectify our foreign policy? I bet not. And just because I feel this way and have the courage of my convictions, I am not unpatriotic and I will not be treated as such.

SALLY: Yes, you will be. If not by me, then by Gloria and Carl and our neighbors and friends, our fellow church members and other relatives. You know how they will treat you. They will treat you as a traitor, a turncoat, someone who says he loves his nephew and stabs him in the back by supporting the enemy. Are you really willing to alienate yourself from your own sister and brother-in-law, the majority of the community, and even from me, for the sake of your opposition to this war?

GEROGE: Be alienated from you, too? Would you really abandon me just because I feel a visceral hatred for this whole awful adventure?

SALLY: *(Pretends to be considering the possibility.)* Well, maybe not me. I know I married a radical free thinker, one of those people who marches to the beat of a different drummer. I might oppose you politically, but I can't stop loving you for being who you are. *(Goes over and gives*

GEORGE *a little kiss and a hug.)* You have a big heart. But sometimes you just have to use your head. *(Knocks his head before returning to her chair.)*

GEORGE: I think I am using my head. And anyway, can't we just use our heart sometimes, too? Can't we just go where our emotions lead us once in awhile?

SALLY: Sure. But remember what Hitler said about that: "Seek me with your heart and not with your head."

GEORGE: You devil! How dare you compare me with Hitler!

SALLY: That's true. It's an unfair comparison. You don't have his mustache. *(Pauses a moment.)* You know, I think you really do love Michael. But sometimes I wonder if your love for him doesn't get in the way of your objectivity.

GEORGE: Why shouldn't I love my own nephew? He's like the son we never had.

SALLY: I know. I know. But he's tall and handsome, with big blue eyes and blond hair. Everyone loves Michael.

GEORGE: Sally! You can just be plain perverse sometimes. I have never considered Michael anything but a nephew, my sister's son. What on earth are you thinking? You can be such a sicko sometimes.

SALLY: I didn't say you loved him that way. But sometimes I wonder. You look at him with such admiration. And besides, if I'm a sicko, at least I'm a practical one and I'm not blind to the complexity of human emotions.

GEORGE: So you think my judgment is impaired because I have a gay incestuous love for my own nephew? Is that what you're trying to say?

SALLY: No. I'm not saying that. But you have to admit that Michael is a very attractive and lovable young man.

GEORGE: Yes. He is attractive. But he's my nephew, for God's sake. I don't have sexual feelings for members of my own family.

SALLY: Not even for me?

GEROGE: For you? Yes, most of the time. But not right now because you're getting on my nerves. *(Pauses.)* And by the way, wouldn't you be only too happy to send Michael off to war to get rid of a potential rival? Doesn't that follow your same twisted logic?

SALLY: Touché, Dr. Freud. *(Laughs, then sits back down and picks up the paper.)* Did you see that Charles De Gaulle finally died?

GEROGE: Really? That's too bad. He was a great statesman and a great French patriot.

SALLY: Yeah. Couldn't have happened to a nicer guy.

GEORGE: Don't be spiteful. He did a lot for France. *(Takes the paper and looks at the article.)*

SALLY: Like what? He certainly didn't liberate France without our help, regardless of what he said.

GEORGE: Well, he did have the courage to get France out of Algeria despite a lot of internal opposition. He even risked assassination attempts. Maybe Kissinger and Nixon can learn a lesson or two and get us out of Vietnam?

SALLY: Vietnam! Vietnam! Vietnam! My God, you sound like a broken record sometimes. Can't you think about anything else these days? *(Laughs and looks down at her watch.)* Look at the time. We better get going if we're supposed be there by noon.

(GEORGE and SALLY get up and leave the table. As they do, they take the cups, coffee and newspaper with them. Lights dim to dark.)

THE END

THE PERFECT HOUSE

CAST OF CHARACTERS

MARGARET FAIRCLOTH: Well dressed middle aged woman. She wears a lot of flashy silver jewelry.

JAKE WHITECLOUD: Middle aged Native American man, dressed in a flannel shirt, overalls, and dirty boots. He wears his salt and pepper hair in a pony tail and a floppy hat with a feather in it.

SETTING

The set is stark. There are only a couple of posts, suggestive of a billboard poles. Jake, who has a brush and a bucket of paint, is painting the post during the play.

MARGARET: I've got to talk to you.

JAKE: What's up, ma'am?

MARGARET: Trouble

JAKE: What kinda trouble?

MARGARET: (*Points up to the imaginary billboard.*) This kind of trouble!

JAKE: It's just a billboard.

MARGARET: Of course it's a billboard. I can see that. It's also blocking my $50,000 view of the Willamette Valley.

JAKE: So?

MARGARET: So! I paid a million dollars to build that house over there on the hill and I don't want to look out my living room window and see a billboard for Harley-Davidson motorcycles. I'm an artist and it offends my artistic sensibilities. I can't create when I see this obstruction.

JAKE: Ever owned a Harley, ma'am?

MARGARET: (*Looks at JAKE incredulously.*) No! This is not about a particular product; it's about that hideous monstrosity of a billboard blocking my view.

JAKE: (*Returns to so some painting on the post.*) Sorry, ma'am. But it's my land and that guy down at the county office told me I could put it up. Just so long as it ain't higher than 40 feet. (*Turns toward MARGARET.*) And it's only 35.

MARGARET: I don't believe you. They have got to have some restrictions in this place. No one would allow you to defile this paradise with this nightmare.

JAKE: (*Shrugs.*) Suit yourself. (*Pulls out a cell phone and dials.*) Here, talk to Mr. Chadwick at the county office.

MARGARET: (*Takes the phone.*) Hello. This is Margaret Faircloth. Yes. Yes, I'm doing fine. Thank you. Yes, I like my new house. (*Pauses.*) But I don't like this giant billboard my neighbor put up. His name? (*Turns to Jake.*) What's your name?

JAKE: Jake. Jake Whitecloud.

MARGARET: (*Speaks in the phone.*) Whitecloud. Jake Whitecloud. (*Frowns*). I see. I see. Thank you. (*Hands the phone back to JAKE.*) Apparently they have no zoning restrictions out here.

JAKE: Told you.

MARGARET: (*Looks up at the billboard.*) Whitecloud. That's Native American, isn't it?

JAKE: Yes, ma'am.

MARGARET: I thought Native Americans were supposed to be one with the land and all that.

JAKE: We are one with the land.

MARGARET: (*Speaks angrily.*) Then how does this ugly monstrosity fit in with being one with the land. It's a horror. It's a sacrilege. It's an insult to this landscape. (*Makes a wide gesture with her hand.*)

JAKE: (*Looks up at the billboard.*) I like motorcycles. You sit on a big Harley and go roarin' down the road. It's like you're flyin' like an eagle. I can feel my ancestors ridin' along with me. They rise from the dead and ride with me.

MARGARET: (*Looks at JAKE with concern.*) You're kidding me, aren't you?

JAKE: (*Ignores her question and looks at the billboard.*) There! Look at those beautiful machines. They're gleamin' in the sun.

MARGARET: They're blocking my view. And they're blocking my artistic juices.

JAKE: (*Continues to ignore MARGARET.*) My mother used to tell me stories about my father. He was a great man. His name was Screamin' Eagle, just the same as those motorcycles. Screamin' Eagles. When I found that out, I knew he had come back from the grave to be with me. (*Points up again.*) All that chrome and leather, those pipes and pistons. Those machines pulse. They throb. They rumble and lurch forward. (*Gestures toward MARGARET.*) They grab the road like a man grabs a woman. (*Grabs MARGARET, who backs up.*) You wanna ride a Harley with me?

MARGARET: (*Screams.*) No! Get your hands off me! Get your face out of my face! And get this billboard out of my view! (*Pushes JAKE to the ground.*)

JAKE: (*Stands up calmly and brushes himself off.*) You seem so tense, so filled with anger? Why are you so angry?

MARGARET: (*Straightens out her clothing.*) I'm angry because I came here to be one with nature, one with the universe, one with God. I wanted the perfect house in the perfect place with the perfect view. I wanted to live in artistic perfection so I could create art that would also be perfect. (*Pauses and points up.*) And you and your billboard spoiled everything. This is a rape of the land, an intrusion of commercialism, a horrible blot on this pristine landscape. How can you tolerate that, even if your father's name was Screamin' Eagle? (*Pauses.*) You're a traitor. You're a traitor to your people and a traitor to this place.

JAKE: (*Makes a sweeping gesture.*) This entire valley belonged to my people. All of this land as far as the eye can see. My father and his father and his father's father lived here. We hunted and fished and farmed where we pleased. (*Drops his hands.*) Now I have a half an acre and a trailer. I live on a $500 pension check every month.

MARGARET: A pension for what?

JAKE: I got wounded in Vietnam. Shot in the stomach.

MARGARET: I'm sorry.

JAKE: No need. (*Continues to paint.*)

MARGARET: (*Points to the billboard.*) How much do you get for this billboard?

JAKE: A thousand dollars a year.

MARGARET: I'll pay. I'll give you the same amount of money to take it down.

JAKE: No.

MARGARET: Why?

JAKE: Because I don't want your money.

MARGARET: What do you want?

JAKE: I want you.

MARGARET: (*Looks astonished.*) Me? (*Studies JAKE as he speaks.*)

JAKE: (*Sets down the brush.*) I've seen you up there in your glass house; all lit up like a Christmas tree. (*Mimics sensual movements.*) You wander around half-naked in your Victoria Secret outfits, while I sit down here and look up there at you. You look like you're screamin' out for a man. And it's like we were a million miles apart, not just a few hundred yards. (*Points off.*) Right there, right where you built your house on the hill, my mother used to take me to look for wild strawberries. It was pristine then. It was beautiful then. It was sure a lot better than with your big old house. (*Pauses.*) Why shouldn't I put up a billboard? Do your really blame me? Who wrecked what around here?

MARGARET: Do you really want me? That way?

JAKE: Yes. I do.

MARGARET: (*Ponders a little and then holds out her arms.*) Then take me! Let me feel the intensity of your desire. Let me feel the surge of your Native American body in mine. I'll finally be one with nature, one with the land, one with the son of the Great Spirit. Maybe that's what I've been looking for all along, the perfect relationship to fuel my creative energies, not the perfect house. I've been so blind.

JAKE: Can we ride my Screamin' Eagle afterwards.

MARGARET: Anything, Mr. Whitecloud. I'm ready. I'm yours.

(JAKE sets down his brush and turns away and begins drawing on the ground. MARGARET walks over and studies JAKE.)

MARGARET: Are those sacred symbols?

JAKE: Sort of.

MARGARET: It looks like a bird. What is it?

JAKE: An eagle held to the sacred hill by a golden thread of light.

MARGARET: What sacred hill?

JAKE: *(Points to the distance.)* There.

MARGARET: But that's my house.

JAKE: Yes. The same hill, where my mother and me picked strawberries, that's the sacred hill. All my ancestors are held to this land by golden threads that attach to that sacred hill. Then you built your house. Right there on top. And the ancestors are confused and lost.

MARGARET: That's awful. What happens now?

JAKE: Their spirits are doomed to roam the earth and never know the peace and security of their own land. *(Turns to MARGARET.)* You block their spirits from knowing any happiness after death. You never asked me or anyone here if that was a good place to build. Who exactly has committed the greatest desecration, the worse sacrilege? You with your house on the sacred hill? Or me with my Harley-Davidson billboard?

MARGARET: *(Takes JAKE's hand.)* I'm so sorry.

JAKE: This billboard acts as a sign for the spirits. It tells them where the sacred hill is located. It's a roadway, not just billboard. That's why I don't want any money for it. (*Looks at MARGARET.*) Can you live with it, now?

MARGARET: Of course. Of course I can. This changes everything. (*Looks away at MARGARET's house.*) But you can't expect me to tear down my house, can you?

JAKE: No, just leave a light on outside, a yellow one, day and night. That light and the billboard will help guide the spirits when they get confused.

MARGARET: (*Sighs and looks up at the billboard.*) Yes. I can live with it now. (*Looks at JAKE.*) Do you still want me, in my not-so-perfect house on your sacred hill?

JAKE: Yes.

MARGARET: Is there anything else I need to do?

JAKE: Yes. Please join me in a magic dance, like the storks by the river. Then we can go to your house and our bodies and our spirits will be one.

(*JAKE leads MARGARET in an improvised line dance, with some stomping and turning. JAKE sings as they dance. Both smile and laugh. When they finish, they continue to hold hands.*)

MARGARET: Was that a sacred dance you learned from your ancestors?

JAKE: No. It's some steps I picked up from watchin' "Dancin' with the Stars." Let's go.

(*They leave the stage together, hand in hand. The paintbrush and pot of paint remain on the stage. Lights out.*)

THE END

PETS, PEDOPHILES AND POLITICIANS

CAST OF CHARCTERS (IN ORDER OF APPEARANCE)

PRISCILLA SMITH: Evacuee, an older woman, shabbily dressed, but clean.

JERRY MEUNIER: Young man with a past. Casually dressed in a black leather jacket and jeans.

BUS DRIVER

POLICE OFFICER: State Trooper

EDWIN GREER: State politician. May be wearing a sport jacket, no tie.

PATRICK RALSTON: Evacuee shelter manager, casually dressed, no tie.

There are three scenes, which can be played independently or together. If they are played together, they will require six characters.

SCENE I: PETS

CAST OF CHARACTERS (Scene I)

PRISCILLA: An older woman in neat, but shabby, clothing. She is holding a pet carrying case in her lap. She is wearing a white wrist band.

JERRY: A young man casually dressed in a black leather jacket, which covers his red wrist band.

BUS DRIVER: May be black or white. He has a cap or something to indicate his job.

SETTING

The set is very simple. There are a few rows of chairs lined up to indicate seats on a bus. They are facing the audience. Priscilla and Jerry are initially seated side by side on the first set of chairs.

BUS DRIVER: (*Confronts PRISCILLA.*) You gotta get rid of that dog, Lady.

PRISCILLA: I can't. Cory is my life. He's my only friend, my only family. I can't leave Cory behind to die. The whole city is supposed to flood. Where would we go?

DRIVER: Listen, Lady. I don't care. They told us there was not supposed to be any animals on this bus, just people. And this is my bus and we can't have an animals stinking up this vehicle any more than it already is.

PRISCILLA: Cory doesn't smell. She's a very clean dog. (*Sniffs the cage.*) Here, smell. (*Lifts up the cage to the DRIVER.*)

DRIVER: (*Sniffs.*) Smells like a dog to me, a wet one. (*Shakes his head.*) The rules is the rules. No animals on this bus or I ain't leavin'. No one goes anywhere until your dog is outta here. If you wanna get off with your mutt, that's your business, but do it now.

JERRY: Leave the lady alone!

DRIVER: Keep your nose outta this, mister, or you're goin' off too.

JERRY: (*Stands up and confronts the DRIVER.*) I said leave her alone! That dog ain't botherin' anybody.

DRIVER: It's against the rules, it's botherin' me!

JERRY: Then we'll move back a few rows and you won't have to deal with it so close up and personal. How about that?

DRIVER: Front, back, it don't make no difference. I'm not leavin' until that dog's outta here and I want it off now!

PRISCILLA: Please, mister. I can't leave my dog behind. I'll get off. We'll stay behind. I don't care if we both drown.

JERRY: (*Pushes PRISCILLA gently back down in her seat.*) Sit down. You can't stay behind. You might not even have a house to go back to. We gotta evacuate and we're leavin' together, dog and all.

DRIVER: Are you guys related?

PRISCILLA: No.

JERRY: (*Interrupts PRISCILLA.*) Yes. This is my auntie. We're related. And I'm takin' responsibility. (*Reaches in his wallet and pulls out some bills and presents them to the DRIVER.*) And maybe this'll make you forget that the dog's on this bus.

DRIVER: (*Looks at the money, hesitates and then takes it and stuffs it in his pocket.*) Move back a couple of rows and don't let nobody see that damned dog.

(*PRISCILLA and JERRY move back a couple of rows and settle in.*)

PRISCILLA: Thank you, young man.

JERRY: It's okay. (*Looks at the cage.*) What kinda of a dog is it?

(*PRISCILLA opens the cage. There does not need to be a real dog in the cage.*)

PRISCILLA: Cory's a Pekinese-mix. (*She looks at JERRY.*) You wanna pet her?

JERRY: Does she bite?

PRISCILLA: No. She's as gentle as a lamb. Besides, she doesn't have any teeth any more. Like me.

JERRY: (*Puts his hand in the cage and appears to be stroking the dog.*) Wow. She's so nice and soft. (*Closes his eyes and continues to stroke.*) Hmmm. Soft as a baby's hair.

PRISCILLA: (*Looks alarmed.*) That's enough. (*Closes the door to the cage.*) She gets a little nervous if she gets too much petting. (*Notices JERRY has a red wrist band.*) What's that?

JERRY: My identification arm band.

PRISCILLA: But it's red. Mine's white. (*Shows JERRY her wrist band.*)

JERRY: Yeah. (*Takes out a pocket knife and cuts off the band, and then puts the knife and the band in his jacket pocket.*)

PRISCILLA: I thought we were supposed to keep them bands on the whole trip, to keep track of everyone.

JERRY: Yeah.

PRISCILLA: Why's yours red?

(*JERRY shrugs his shoulders.*)

PRISCILLA: Are you some sorta criminal?

JERRY: No.

PRISCILLA: Then what are you?

JERRY: Do you really wanna know?

PRISCILLA: (*Pauses.*) Yes.

JERRY: I'm a registered sex offender.

PRISCILLA: (*Backs away.*) Really? (*Clutches her cage and starts to stand up.*)

JERRY: Don't worry, it's just with children.

PRISCILLA: (*Raises her voice.*) Just with children!

JERRY: Shhhhhh! Not so loud, please.

PRISCILLA: But that's terrible.

JERRY: That's what my mom says, too. Go ahead, you can move away from me. I'm used to it.

PRISCILLA: (*Starts to move, then hesitates and sits down.*) But children?

JERRY: It was mostly pictures on the computer and that sort of thing. I never really touched any kids. Not to say I didn't want to. But I got my principles, too.

PRISCILLA: So your family rejected you.

JERRY: (*Sighs.*) My mom did. I never knew my dad. She found my pictures and videos and kicked me outta the house. So I moved in with this guy who let me stay as long as he could have sex with me. At first it really bothered me, but after awhile I got used to it. He even got me hooked on hard core porn. (*Stops.*) I swear I never touched any kids. I just kind of got addicted to those pictures. Maybe I was just lookin' for somethin' innocent and pure. Nothin' like I'd ever known in my life. I finally wised up and got away from that guy. (*Pauses.*) Can I pet your dog again?

PRISCILLA: (*Looks back and forth between JERRY and the cage.*) Okay. But not too long and not too hard.

JERRY: (*Puts his hand in the cage and pets the dog.*) So soft. So fluffy.

PRISCILLA: (*Slams the door shut.*) Okay, that's enough.

(*They sit in silence for a few seconds.*)

JERRY: Are you goin' turn me in?

PRISCILLA: I should turn you in. (*Nods her head.*)

JERRY: Why?

PRISCILLA: Because you might pose a danger to the children in the shelter where we're goin'.

JERRY: I'm not dangerous. But if you think I am, I'll turn myself in. (*Starts to stand up.*)

PRISCILLA: (*Pulls him down.*) No. Don't go. I won't say nothing.

JERRY: (*Drops back down in his seat.*) Why did you change your mind?

PRISCILLA: Because you helped me with Cory. (*Pauses.*) And because you look like my nephew. You've got the same eyes and the same mouth. I thought about him and I just couldn't let you get sent there with all those perverts. I know what they do to young men in them places.

JERRY: You're right about that. It can be tough. The first time I went to jail, I got raped in the first 12 hours.

PRISCILLA: That's awful.

JERRY: Yeah, it was awful. But it taught me a lot, too.

PRISCILLA: Like what?

JERRY: Like who you needed to know to survive. Which guys could offer you protection in return for, you know.

PRISCILLA: Know what?

JERRY: You know. (*Makes a pumping gesture near his crotch with his hand.*)

PRISCILLA: (*Turns away briefly.*) I think we need to change the subject.

JERRY: Okay. But can I pet your puppy one more time.

PRISCILLA: (*Hesitates again.*) Okay, but just for a little while, and just on the top, okay? No funny business.

JERRY: Okay. (*Puts in his hand and begins to pet. Closes his eyes.*) So soft and gentle. You got a nice dog lady. And you're a nice person, too.

PRISCILLA: Thank you for helpin' me out with my dog. I'm glad I let you stay.

JERRY: Me, too.

  (*Lights out.*)

SCENE II: PEDOPHILES

CAST OF CHARACTERS

PRISCILLA: A middle aged woman, dressed in shabby clothing and carrying a pet carrying case with a dog.

JERRY: A young man with a leather jacket.

POLICE OFFICER: A uniformed police officer.

SETTING

There are a couple of rows of chairs, facing the audience. They represent the rows of seats on a bus. Jerry and Priscilla are seated together in the second or third row of chairs. She holds the dog carrying case on her lap.

(*JERRY sees the officer approaching and he pulls his red arm band out of his pocket and stuffs it into PRISCILLA's purse. PRISCILLA notices what JERRY has done, but does not react.*)

OFFICER: (*To STEVE.*) Where's your arm band?

JERRY: I left it at home.

OFFICER: What's your name?

JERRY: Brian. Brian Hill.

OFFICER: (*Uses a hand held device and checks for the name.*) I don't see anyone by that name in the system. (*Studies JERRY's face.*) In fact, I think I saw you earlier in the group going to the Gonzales shelter.

PRISCILLA: What's the Gonzales Shelter? If it's closer, can I go there, too?

OFFICER: You don't want to go there, ma'am.

PRISCILLA: Why?

OFFICER: It's reserved for perverts.

PRISCILLA: Perverts?

OFFICER: Yeah. Pedophiles, sexual predators, and I think this guy next to you may be one of them.

PRISCILLA: (*Looks astonished.*) Really? I don't believe it.

OFFICER: Why not?

PRISCILLA: Because he's my nephew and his name is Brian, Brian Hill, just like he said.

OFFICER: Really?

PRISCILLA: Yes. He's been staying with me since my daughter died of breast cancer a few months ago. Her death has been so hard on all of us. And Brian has been so helpful. I don't know what I would have done without him. He's been taking care of me and Cory. (*Shows the OFFICER the cage.*) Cory's my Pekinese mix. You want see her?

OFFICER: (*Glances briefly at the dog cage, and then continues speaking to JERRY.*) So what happened to your name band?

JERRY: I don't know. It must have fallen off back in New Orleans.

OFFICER: (*Looks skeptical.*) Okay. Now, what about that dog? I thought there weren't supposed to be any animals on these buses.

JERRY: That's none of your business. Go look for some perverts, not pets.

OFFICER: (*Frowns.*) Okay. But I got my eye on you. (*Points at JERRY and then walks away.*)

JERRY: (*Turns to PRISCILLA.*) Thank you.

PRISCILLA: No problem.

JERRY: You didn't have to stick up for me. Why'd you do that?

PRISCILLA: You helped me with Cory. You stood up for me and my pet. And you do remind me of my nephew. (*Pauses.*) He died of AIDS back in the 80's. At the time, I never accepted him and never said anything nice to him before he died. (*Pauses.*) He didn't deserve to die, especially sick and alone like he did. He was always kind to me and to my dog, like you. He had his own dog, an ugly little mutt, but they made him give it away when his immune system got real bad. It nearly broke his heart. He asked me if I wanted to take his dog and I refused. I thought the dog might be sick, too. It was silly and I never stuck up for him or his dog. They had to put that puppy down. And my nephew died just after that, maybe from a broken heart.

JERRY: I don't have AIDS, if that's what you think.

PRISCILLA: I don't know what you have. But you were kind to my dog. They wanted to kick him off, too. (*Pauses*). You really don't hurt children, do you?

JERRY: No. Just pictures. I just look at pictures and videos. And I don't take them myself. You know, I just look, for the pleasure. I look and I don't touch real kids.

PRISCILLA: It still hurts them, you know. Cause someone else has to take them pictures.

JERRY: I know. But I can't help myself. It's stronger than me. I just look at them sweet little kids and it makes me excited.

PRISCILLA: Stop!

JERRY: Stop what?

PRISCILLA: I don't want to hear any more about it. I just want you to sit here next to me and drive up on to Fulton together to that shelter. And I don't you be thinking of doing anything bad to any children up their either.

JERRY: I wouldn't do that.

PRISCILLA: Cross your heart and hope to die?

JERRY: (*Crosses his heart with a simple back and forth gesture.*) Cross my heart.

PRISCILLA: (*Crosses herself, too, according to the Catholic tradition.*) Me, too.

OFFICER: (*Returns and addresses PRISCILLA.*) Ma'am, with all due respect, I think this guy is Jerry Meunier and I'm taking him off this bus. (*Grabs JERRY.*)

PRISCILLA: (*Pulls on JERRY's other arm.*) No you don't! I'll scream. (*Screams very loudly.*)

OFFICER: (*Continues to pull.*) I'll arrest both of you for resisting arrest. I swear to God I will.

PRISCILLA: (*Starts to hit at the OFFICER's arm.*) Leave him alone! Leave him alone!

JERRY: (*To PRISCILLA.*) It's okay. I'll go. Thanks for trying to help me.

PRISCILLA: (*Grabs her cage.*) I'll let my dog out and she'll bite your ass!

OFFICER: Don't try, lady, or I'll shoot it dead. (*Sits back down and starts to cry. To JERRY.*)

PRISCILLA: Take care of yourself.

JERRY: I will. And you take care of that dog.

PRISCILLA: I will. Good luck. (*Reaches in her purse and pulls out the red arm band. Puts it around her wrist and stands up, still clutching her carrying cage.*) Take me! Take me, too! I'm a pervert, too. See my arm band. It's a red one.

OFFICER: (*Examines the band.*) Yeah. And I guess your name's Jerry Meunier. (*Laughs and throws the arm band on the floor.*) Nice try, lady. Now sit down. This bus is taking off to Fulton.

PRISCILLA: (*Jumps up.*) No!

OFFICER: Sit down, lady! I'm just doin' my job. We've got strict orders, right from the governor's office. We gotta keep these perverts away from the other folks, especially children. It's a question of safety. It's also the law. You should be thankful I'm takin' this creep outta here.

PRISCILLA: No! It's wrong and Jerry's not a creep. He's a decent young man and he helped me and my dog. You can't take him. I'll take care of him. I'll keep an eye out on him. He'll be good. I know he'll be good.

OFFICER: Okay. That's it, you crazy old loon. You're coming with me, too. (*Grabs PRISCILLA with his free hand.*)

PRISCILLA: Good. And you better put me with Jerry so we can look out for one another. (*Clutches her dog cage and her purse as she is being pulled up.*)

OFFICER: (*Leads them both away.*) With Jerry, eh? You wanna be with Jerry so you can look out after each other with all of them sex perverts. (*Laughs.*) Right.

(The OFFICER drags them both off the bus. Lights out.)

SCENE III: POLITICIANS

CAST OF CHARACTERS

EDWIN GREER: Local state representative, dressed in a shirt and slacks.

PATRICK RALSTON: Evacuee shelter manager. He is casually dressed.

PRISCILLA: An older woman evacuee. She is seated on a cot and has a dog carrying case under the cot.

SETTING

There are a few cots that suggest a larger building, full of cots and refugees. Priscilla is lying on her cot. There is one that is free next to hers.

EDWIN: *(Surveys the room.)* Don't these poor people even get real beds?

PATRICK: No sir, they just have cots.

EDWIN: Cots can't be that comfortable for some of these people. I've had several complaints from my constituents about this very issue.

PATRICK: This isn't a resort, sir; it's just an evacuee shelter.

EDWIN: No, of course it's not a resort, but we have an obligation to our constituents. Can you imagine sleeping on something like this?

(*Lies down on the empty cot next to PRISCILLA's.*) My God, it's as hard as a rock.

PATRICK: Yes, they are firm.

EDWIN: These poor folks need some comfort, not this kind of torture.

PATRICK: We can't buy beds, sir. It's totally out of our budget. This is the best we can do with the limited money we have.

EDWIN: Whose budget?

PATRICK: The State's budget, sir.

EDWIN: And who was so cruel as to not allocate adequate funds for this important service?

PATRICK: You, sir.

EDWIN: Me?

PATRICK: Yes. Well, maybe not you personally, but the legislature refused to match funds from the Federal government, so we lost several million dollars. It was taken out of the disaster preparedness funding. You remember?

EDWIN: Ah yes. Perhaps I do. (*Looks down at PRISCILLA, who is lying on her cot.*) What's your name, dear?

PRISCILLA: Priscilla Smith.

EDWIN: (*Extends his hand.*) Hi. I'm Edwin Greer, state representative. I'm here checking on the conditions in the shelter. Are you doing okay?

PRISCILLA: (*Stands up.*) No. I'm not okay. (*Points to her cot.*) This thing is as hard as a rock. And there's no one to take care of my dog. We can't get a decent snack and there's not even any dog food.

EDWIN: You eat dog food?

PRISCILLA: No, silly. For my dog, Cory. (*Pulls her dog carrier out from under her cot and shows it to EDWIN.*) They wanted to take her away from me on the bus, but a nice young man, Mr. Jerry Meunier, made them leave me alone.

EDWIN: (*Leans toward PATRICK.*) Are they supposed to let dogs into the shelter?

PATRICK: No.

EDWIN: Then how did this one get in here?

PATRICK: (*Shrugs his shoulders.*) I don't know.

PRISCILLA: I'll tell you. This nice young man by the name of Jerry Meunier made them let me keep Cory on the bus.

EDWIN: Jerry Meunier? (*Pauses.*) A young man with brown hair and brown eyes, medium build? (*This description may be altered to reflect the actor portraying JERRY.*)

PRISCILLA: Yeah, that's the one. I told them I was his aunt so they wouldn't take him off the bus.

EDWIN: Take him off the bus? Where? Why?

PRISCILLA: (*Leans forward in confidence.*) Because he had a red wrist band.

EDWIN: (*Leans toward PATRICK.*) What does that mean?

PATRICK: (*PATRICK half whispers to EDWIN.*) Pedophile.

EDWIN: What? I can't hear a word you're saying.

PRISCILLA: Jerry said it meant he was a child molester! But he told me he never touched children. He only looked at pictures.

EDWIN: You're lying.

PRISCILLA: I am not!

EDWIN: This woman is lying.

PATRICK: (*Shrugs his shoulders.*) I don't know anything about this, sir, except that this dog shouldn't be here. This is a people shelter, not a pet shelter.

EDWIN: Then get that thing out of here and take this lady, too.

PRISCILLA: I tried to keep them from taking Jerry. I tried to go with him, 'cause he protected my dog and he reminded me of my own nephew who died of AIDS.

EDWIN: This woman and her dog have got to go.

PATRICK: We can't kick her out, sir.

EDWIN: Your told me that the rules are the rules. No animals in a people shelter.

PRISCILLA: And no perverts with children!

EDWIN: There has to have been some sort of mistake. That young man could not have been Jerry Meunier. He's the son of the Margaret Meunier, a charming Christian woman from Pointe Coupée Parish.

PRISCILLA: He tried to help me. He tried to help me and my dog. He didn't do anything wrong and they still took him away.

EDWIN: (*Speaks to PATRICK.*) Where would they have taken him?

PATRICK: To Gonzales. There's a special shelter there for sex offenders.

EDWIN: Who made that sort of decision? It's segregation. It's discrimination.

PATRICK: It's a question of safety, sir. We try and make sure sexual predators are not mixed with children in the general shelters.

PRISCILLA: He said he never touched children. He just looked at the pictures. I told him that was still wrong, but he said it was stronger than him.

EDWIN: Shipping off pedophiles. It's like the Nazis. Who decided on such a thing?

PATRICK: You did?

EDWIN: I did?

PATRICK: Yes, sir. The legislature passed the law last session after incidents which took place in the shelters a couple of years ago. You know, the one with the children in Monroe. It's a public safety issue.

EDWIN: Oh yes. I remember. (*Pauses.*) But Jerry was such a nice boy, a good young man with a very Christian mother. I really admired his mother, a real looker, and we really were in love. And I would have married her, too, if she hadn't got pregnant. And I was still married to my second wife. I just couldn't dump her and recognize the boy and have any hope of being re-elected. (*Pauses.*) That good-for-nothing creep down there in St. Francisville was the only one she could get to marry her before the baby was born. I guess it would have been okay, but that guy wasn't a Saint Joseph. He beat her, and the kid, too. I never got to know Jerry and all. His mom always told Jerry that this other guy wasn't his real father. He was such a nice little boy. I just couldn't acknowledge him and get re-elected. You know what I mean?

PATRICK: And now? What's different?

EDWIN: Well, I'm term limited now, so it doesn't make any difference. Unless I run for the senate next time. (*Pauses.*) He was such a good boy.

PRISCILLA: I thought he was a nice boy, too. I told the police that he was my nephew so they wouldn't take him or my dog away. I tried to help him. And he really liked Cory, my dog.

EDWIN: (*Looks at the cage.*) Yes, of course, the dog.

PATRICK: Yes, sir, the one that should be in the special pet shelter someplace else.

EDWIN: (*To PRISCILLA.*) Did Jerry seem upset when they took him away?

PRISCILLA: No, not at the end. He just let them lead him away. He looked kinda sad, but not really upset. Like he kinda half expected it. He still didn't want to go, 'cause he said the other guys might take advantage of him. I wanted the police man to take me too, but they just put me back on another bus headed for Fulton.

PATRICK: (*Picks up the dog carrier.*) Ma'am, we gotta get rid of this dog. Not permanently, just for a little while. He needs to go in a special shelter for pets.

PRISCILLA: (*Starts to cry.*) Don't take my puppy. Cory's all I got. I can't stand to be without her. Please, mister. Don't take my dog away from me.

EDWIN: Leave the dog alone!

PATRICK: But you said it had to go.

EDWIN: I know what I said. And I can also change my mind. So leave the dog here. And get me the numbers of that place down in Gonzales. I've got to get Jerry out of there.

PATRICK: But he's there because he's supposed to be. They're just following the rules.

EDWIN: Damn the rules.

PATRICK: I'm paid to follow the rules you made, sir.

EDWIN: Well, I'm telling you to let the dog stay. And get this woman a decent mattress or an egg crate, or anything to soften this cot. Who could sleep on something like this, anyway?

PATRICK: Yes, sir.

EDWIN: And don't forget to get me the name and address of the person in charge down in Gonzales. I've got to make a trip down there.

PATRICK: Yes, sir. Right away, sir.

EDWIN: (*Returns the cage to PRISCILLA.*) Here, lady. Take your dog and keep it quiet. And thank you for trying to help out Jerry. He's a good boy. And I really loved his mother. But politics is politics. (*Turns and walks briskly away with PATRICK trailing along.*) And don't forget to remind me to talk about keeping people and their pets together during evacuations from now on. It's inhuman to separate a person from their pet. They've already lost everything and we make them give up their pets, too? It's inhuman. It's anti-American. It's an outrage and I intend to make of change of policy as soon as I get back to Baton Rouge.

(*EDWIN strides off the stage. Lights out.*)

THE END

PROFIT, PASSION AND POLITICS

This is a play in three scenes. Each scene may be played independently. The number of characters will depend on whether it is done as a unit or separately.

CAST OF CHARCTERS (IN ORDER OF APPEARANCE)

ERNIE CORTEZ: Plaintiff's attorney, middle-aged, well-dressed.

PATRICIA WELLS: Client, middle-aged woman, shabbily dressed.

PAUL VERRET: Defense attorney.

JUDGE BANKS: An older man, dressed in a judge's robe.

SCENE I: PROFIT

CAST OF CHARACTERS

ERNIE CORTEZ: Plaintiff's attorney, a well-dressed but sleazy character.

PATRICIA WELLS: Prospective client in a medication class-action suit.

SETTING

There is a desk with some papers and an intercom and a couple of chairs. Mr. Cortez is seated at the desk. Mrs. Wells is in a chair in front of the desk. There is a shiny imitation silver crucifix on the wall. It should be obvious and well lit.

PATRICIA: I don't like the idea.

ERNIE: What's there not to like about it, Mrs. Wells?

PATRICIA: I didn't actually have a heart attack because of the medication I took; I think it was really due to my smoking and bad diabetes.

ERNIE: Who cares what actually caused it? You had a documented heart attack. Don't you want to get some of the thousands of dollars out there, just yours for the taking? (*Gets up and walks around the desk and addresses PATRICIA.*) Think of that little condo you always wanted down in South Beach. Or that place up in the mountains you could only dream about. Think about paying off your mortgage or helping your grand children with their college tuition.

PATRICIA: That all sounds great, but is it honest?

ERNIE: Honest? Honest? Of course it's honest. Thousands of lawyers all over the country are helping their clients get what they deserve.

PATRICIA: But what if I don't deserve it?

ERNIE: (*Pauses and frowns.*) Maybe you don't deserve it, but I certainly do.

PATRICIA: (*Looks at ERNIE skeptically.*) Why should I do this for you?

ERNIE: Very simple. Because I get thirty-five percent of the settlement, Mrs. Wells.

PATRICIA: That's a very honest thing to say.

ERNIE: I told you I'm an honest person. And I think that's the number one reason you should trust me.

PATRICIA: But thirty-five percent for you, that's a lot of money.

ERNIE: It certainly is. And multiply that by the hundreds clients I hope to get together, if I'm lucky.

PATRICIA: That could represent a fortune.

ERNIE: I hope so. (*Pauses.*) But please remember, Mrs. Wells, this is NOT about the money. (*Pauses.*) It's about justice. It's about sending a message to those big greedy drug companies that they cannot endanger the public by hiding data and lying in a quest to increase their stock holder's profit margins. Now that's a crime, a real crime.

PATRICIA: And if I lie to make us both rich, isn't that a crime, too?

ERNIE: (*Comes over and puts his hand on PATRICIA's shoulder.*) It's not the same thing at all. We're just poor humble citizens trying to right the wrongs of this evil society. Neither of us are multi-million dollar corporations, are we?

PATRICIA: No, but I just don't feel right about it.

ERNIE: Trust me, not your feelings. I will come through for you, (*Pauses*) for us. I will stand by you now that you have been abandoned by the whole world. (*Pauses again and looks at the crucifix.*) You remind me so much of my saintly departed mother. I could never really help her since she died so young, but you, Mrs. Wells, you can receive the full benefits of my love and generosity. You can profit from my knowledge of the law, unlike my deceased mother. (*Glances at the cross and crosses himself.*) May her soul rest in peace.

PATRICIA: (*Crosses herself as well.*) But what about my nephew, Greg?

ERNIE: Greg? (*Looks startled.*) Did he take the same medication you did? Did he have a heart attack?

PATRICIA: No, of course not. He's way too young for that. But he does work for the drug company that makes it. He says this class action lawsuit might put them out of business and he might lose his job.

ERNIE: (*Thinks for a moment.*) I feel sorry for Greg. I really do. But you have to think about yourself, Mrs. Wells. Is your nephew Greg going to take care of you in your old age? Are Greg and his drug company employer going to get you into a nursing home and pay the bills when you're too sick to stay in your own home?

PATRICIA: He might. He's a good boy, even if he's a bit strange. (*Leans in to speak to ERNIE.*) I think he might be gay.

ERNIE: (*Raises his hands to the heavens in a gesture of supplication.*) His sexual orientation is of no interest to me. But as far as taking care of you in your old age, I tell you, gay or straight, he will not!

PATRICIA: How do you know?

ERNIE: I, myself, have experienced the full brunt of filial ingratitude. My own children have turned against me after I showered them with generosity: cars, college educations, vacations, fancy clothing and jewelry, even houses. And not one of them still speaks to me. (*Pauses and looks heavenward.*) And if they do call, it's just to ask for money. (*Looks around.*) Not one of them remembers my birthday or Father's Day. No, they just call me for cash. And when, in my goodness, I give them some, I never get so much as a thank you. It's a sin, I tell you, a real tragedy.

PATRICIA: Your own children really treat you like that?

ERNIE: Yes, it's true. (*Pauses.*) And, trust me; your nephew Greg will be no different. (*Glances at his watch and then looks at PATRICIA.*) So may I assume that you will go forward with the case? I really must have a response.

PATRICIA: But Greg. What will happen to him if he loses his job, his apartment? He might end up unemployed, depressed, and maybe even homeless.

ERNIE: You can buy him a condo if you want. Or just share some of the money you'll get from the settlement.

PATRICIA: And if I go to hell for lying?

ERNIE: Please, please, please. We are not lying. You took the medication. You had a heart attack. Whether you smoked and had diabetes or not is simply irrelevant. (*Pauses.*) I don't want you to betray your conscience. No. I want you to be at peace with your conscience, just like I am with mine. (*Looks at the crucifix, and then goes down on his knees and pulls the startled PATRICIA down to join him.*) Let's pray together. (*Clasps his hands, closes his eyes and looks heavenward.*) Dear Lord, please grant Sister Wells the courage and wisdom to make the right decision about this important matter. Please give her the peace that comes with being an agent of justice in this troubled and sinful world. Let her doubts and concerns drift away so we may proceed with this case and punish her transgressors in a court of law.

PATRICIA: (*Keeps her eyes closed.*) And Greg? Can we pray for Greg, too?

ERNIE: (*Looks at her, obviously annoyed.*) And let Greg see the errors of his ways, not only in his life style, but in his work for those agents of the devil. Let him come to you, oh Lord, and taste the sweetness of your divine forgiveness that you give to all who come to you with a contrite heart.

PATRICIA: (*Keeps her eyes closed.*) And you and your family? What about them?

ERNIE: (*Scowls and shakes his head.*) And let us pray for my prodigal children, who have also strayed from your holy ways. Let them come home and taste the full goodness of your generosity and mine. Let them see the errors of their evil, ungrateful ways. And let dear Sister Wells accept your will and sign on to this class action suit. Let me become like an angel with a flaming swords of justice and smite those who's greedy hearts have turned away from your divine justice and harmed your innocent lamb, Sister Wells. (*Pauses, glances at his watch, and continues hurriedly.*) And may your will be done. In the name of the Father, the Son, and the Holy Ghost, amen.

PATRICIA: Amen. (*Opens her eyes.*)

(*They both cross themselves while looking at the crucifix and then ERNIE assists PATRICIA up. She seems to be thinking about the situation.*)

PATRICIA: Do you really think this lawsuit is God's will?

ERNIE: Oh yes, no doubt about it. We are both agents of divine justice, Sister Wells.

PATRICIA: Okay, Brother Ernie, if it's the will of God, then let's get those greedy bastards and smite them with God's awful power.

ERNIE: (*Grabs PATRICIA and gives her a big hug.*) That's the spirit! Let's do it! (*Releases PATRICIA and leads her off stage.*) My secretary is waiting in the next office for you to sign the necessary paperwork. It will just take a few seconds.

(*PATRICIA goes out. ERNIE goes to the wall and returns to his desk where he stashes the cross and pulls out a bottle of Jack Daniels. ERNIE pours himself a big glass, which he raises to the ceiling.*)

ERNIE: To my heath, wealth and happiness! (*Downs the glass in a single swallow, and then replaces the glass and bottle in the drawer.*)

(*ERNIE withdraws a menorah, which he places prominently on his desk. He examines a list, and then punches the intercom.*)

ERNIE: Please send in number 247. That would be Mrs. Henrietta Goldstein.

(*Lights out.*)

SCENE II: PASSION

CAST OF CHARACTERS

ERNIE CORTEZ: Plaintiff's attorney, dressed in a flashy suit.

PAUL VERRET: Defense attorney for the pharmaceutical company, also well-dressed in an expensive suit.

PATRICIA WELLS: Shabbily dressed middle-aged woman.

JUDGE BANKS: Presiding judge, dressed in his official robe.

SETTING

There is a slightly raised platform with a chair where the judge sits. In front are a few chairs representing the courtroom. The witness chair is adjacent to the judge's chair and Mrs. Wells is seated there. The audience is the "jury." The two lawyers address the jury.

ERNIE: (*Addresses the audience/jury.*) Ladies and gentleman of the jury, look at this poor woman. She has been reduced from a vibrant, outgoing woman to a physical wreak, a shadow of her former self. She used to walk, play tennis, and even climb mountains. Now she can barely walk across the room while gasping for breath. (*Points to PATRICIA, who slumps down in her chair.*) Now look at her! Just look at her! All this destruction was caused by the corporate greed of a drug company. (*Pauses.*) What kind of a company would sacrifice the life of an innocent woman to satisfy their insatiable appetite for money? Money, money and more money! (*Pauses.*) You have a sacred obligation to send a message to these monsters of greed, these destroyers of lives, these evil social parasites. Help me send that message! Help me give Mrs. Wells some fragment of peace of mind and body. Help me give this woman what she deserves, justice!

JUDGE: Mr. Cortez, do you have any additional questions for your client?

ERNIE: No, Your Honor. (*Takes a seat.*)

JUDGE: Mr. Verret, I believe it's your turn.

PAUL: (*Stands and approaches PATRICIA.*) Hello, Mrs. Wells. My name is Paul Verret and I represent the pharmaceutical company which made the medicine in question. Your doctors have presented evidence that you did, indeed, suffer from a heart attack. (*Pauses.*) How are you feeling now, Mrs. Wells?

PATRICIA: I'm okay, but not like I was before the heart attack.

PAUL: I'm sorry to hear that, Mrs. Wells. By the way, do you smoke?

PATRICIA: Yes.

PAUL: How much?

PATRICIA: Before the heart attack or now?

PAUL: Either one.

PATRICIA: Before my heart attack I used to smoke two packs a day. Now I cut back to only one a day.

PAUL: One cigarette?

PATRICIA: No, only one pack.

PAUL: I see. And how many years have you smoked?

PATRICIA: Twenty, maybe thirty years.

PAUL: Do you know that smoking contributes to heart disease?

ERNIE: (*Jumps up.*) I object! How can the witness be expected to know complex medical subtleties?

PAUL: Your Honor, It is general knowledge that there is an association between cigarette smoking and heart disease. I don't think that's a complex medical subtlety.

JUDGE: Over ruled. Please sit down, Mr. Cortez.

(*ERNIE sits down.*)

PAUL: So you knew that cigarette smoking was not good for you?

PATRICIA: Yes. I think so.

PAUL: How did you know that?

PATRICIA: Because my doctor told me each time I saw him and because Mr. Cortez, my attorney, told me so, too.

ERNIE: I object! This is not relevant information.

JUDGE: Sustained. (*Addresses PAUL.*) I do not think this case is about how Mrs. Wells gained her medical knowledge, but about your client's medication and its effect on her health.

PAUL: (*Addresses the audience/jury.*) I sympathize with Mrs. Wells. I am very sorry that she has any serious medical conditions. But I think you can understand that the motives in this case have little to do about health and everything to do about money. Mr. Cortez is correct that greed is involved here, but it is not corporate greed, it is personal greed. Mrs. Wells is clearly being manipulated to satisfy Mr. Cortez's insatiable greed, not that of my company.

ERNIE: I object. I am not on trial here, nor is my client. The drug company is on trial.

JUDGE: Sustained. (*Addresses the audience/jury.*) Please disregard Mr. Verret's last comments. (*Looks at the attorneys.*) Would you both approach the bench?

(*ERNIE and PAUL approach the bench.*)

JUDGE: You two are to stop with this personal mudslinging regardless of your arguments and their merit or lack thereof. (*Addresses PAUL.*) And you may continue questioning, Mr. Verret, but restrain yourself, please.

PAUL and ERNIE: Yes, Your Honor.

PAUL: (*Returns to question PATRICIA.*) I believe you also have diabetes, Mrs. Wells.

PATRICIA: Yes.

PAUL: How long have you had diabetes?

PATRICIA: Awhile.

PAUL: How long exactly?

PATRICIA: A couple of years.

PAUL: In your deposition, you state that you have suffered from diabetes for the last 12 years. Is that correct?

PATRICIA: (*Shrugs.*) I guess so.

PAUL: And how well would you say you have controlled your diabetes?

PATRICIA: Pretty good.

PAUL: I believe that your medical records shows that your have maintained a glycosylated hemoglobin of around 9%. Is that true?

PATRICIA: I guess it's true if it comes from my chart.

ERNIE: (*To JUDGE.*) I object! How could Mrs. Wells know about such things, she is a patient, not a physician?

PAUL: (*To JUDGE.*) Such information is general knowledge and used by diabetics and their physicians to track their long term diabetic control.

JUDGE: Over ruled. You may continue, Mr. Verret.

PAUL: (*To PATRICIA.*) Do you know what a glycolsylated hemoglobin of 9% means?

PATRICIA: Not exactly, but I know it's bad.

PAUL: How do you know that?

PATRICIA: Because my doctor told me it should be seven percent or less.

PAUL: (*To the jury/audience.*) Just to put things in perspective, a glycosylated hemoglobin of 9% or so corresponds to fasting blood sugars from 350 to 400 most of the time. (*To PATRICIA.*) What did your doctor say was a good fasting blood sugar level?

PATRICIA: Oh, 100 or less.

PAUL: Yes, that is correct. (*Pauses.*) So you were supposed to maintain a blood sugar of 100 or less and your sugars were three to four times higher than that most of the time. Mrs. Wells, did you follow your diet and take your medication in a regular way?

ERNIE: (*To JUDGE.*) I object! Not maintaining a decent blood sugar level just shows that the doctor was not doing his job.

PAUL: (*To JUDGE.*) Your Honor, my understanding was that any medical treatment is a collaboration between the physician and the patient.

JUDGE: Over ruled. That is my understanding as well. You may proceed, Mr. Verret.

PAUL: (*To PATRICIA.*) I noticed in your records that your doctor recommended that you lose at least twenty pounds and that you follow a strict diabetic diet. Did you follow your doctor's instructions regarding your diet and weight control?

PATRICIA: I did the best I could.

PAUL: Did you lose weight during the five years you were with your current doctor?

PATRICIA: I tried.

PAUL: Did you lose weight?

PATRICIA: No.

PAUL: Did you gain weight?

PATRICIA: Yes.

ERNIE: (*To JUDGE.*) I object! Harassing the patient about her weight is not relevant or warranted in this case.

PAUL: (*To JUDGE.*) On the contrary, Your Honor. It is very relevant. Mrs. Wells's noncompliance contributed significantly more to her heart problems than my client's medications.

JUDGE: Over-ruled.

PAUL: (*To PATRICIA.*) Do you know that poorly controlled diabetes contributes to heart disease and that heart disease causes heart attacks?

ERNIE: (*To JUDGE.*) I object! Mrs. Wells does not have the level of physiological knowledge to answer that question, nor should she be expected to answer it.

JUDGE: Over-ruled. Let's hear what Mrs. Wells has to say.

PATRICIA: My doctor told me over and over again that diabetes was bad for my heart, my kidneys, my nerves, and my eyes. He told me that I had to follow a strict diet and lose weight or else my medications would not work, no matter how much I took.

PAUL: (*To jury/audience.*) This is a good woman, a very pleasant and sympathetic woman. But by smoking and not controlling her diet or her weight, she set herself up for an eventual heart attack. My client's medications played no role in this tragic story. (*To PATRICIA.*) I wish we could restore your health, Mrs. Wells. I feel grief for your debilitated condition. But first, I do not believe my client's medications were at fault and second, I do not really think money will help you restore your ravaged health.

PATRICIA: Money might help. And Mr. Cortez says your company has plenty of it for everyone.

PAUL: That's all. Thank you.

JUDGE: Mr. Cortez. Do you have any last questions?

ERNIE: (*Hops up.*) You understand, Mrs. Wells, that this is not about the money, it's about justice.

PATRICIA: Yes, justice not money. That's what you said.

ERNIE: You understand that Mrs. Verret's drug company released a medication to treat your diabetes, but which actually increased your risk for heart attack?

PATRICIA: Yes.

ERNIE: You also understand that the monsters represented here by Mr. Verret have robbed you of your health, your independence, and your very future.

PATRICIA: Yes.

ERNIE: You further understand that the same company has a responsibility, a duty, an obligation to give you back a fraction of the enormous wealth they have stolen from the American people with total disregard for all the rules of decency and a lack of an shred of corporate consciousness.

PAUL: I object! This is slander, nothing more or less.

JUDGE: Sustained. Mr. Cortez, please refrain from gratuitous editorial comments.

ERNIE: Your Honor, no further questions. I trust in the intelligence and wisdom of the ladies and gentlemen of the jury to help us obtain the justice that my long-suffering client so richly deserves.

(*Lights out.*)

SCENE III: POLITICS

CAST OF CHARACTERS

JUDGE BANKS: Not currently dressed in his robes.

ERNIE: Plaintiff's attorney in an expensive imported suit.

SETTING

The Judge is seated at a desk and Ernie is speaking to him. There are a couple of chairs in front of the desk that Ernie may sit in from time to time. The judge is in a suit and tie, his judicial robes hangs on a coat rack.

ERNIE: This has nothing to do with my medication liability case, of course. I just wanted to talk about your re-election campaign.

JUDGE: You had best separate the two issues, Ernie. I don't want to be associated with even the perception of impropriety in any case.

ERNIE: Impropriety? Me? I am like Caesar's wife, above suspicion.

JUDGE: Do you really expect me to believe that, Ernie? (*Pauses.*) So what do you want?

ERNIE: (*Pulls out a check.*) How about a little contribution to your re-election campaign?

JUDGE: (*Looks at the check.*) This is a considerable sum.

ERNIE: You deserve it, Judge. Our firm has been very pleased with your judicial objectivity. (*Pauses.*) You'll note that this check is from our firm, not from me personally.

JUDGE: I hope so.

ERNIE: Of course.

JUDGE: What exactly can I do for you today?

ERNIE: Absolutely nothing. (*Pauses.*) But I would like to discuss some theoretical considerations. (*Gets up and wanders around.*) I have heard some radical rumblings about a sinister movement to appoint judges rather than elect them.

JUDGE: Appoint judges?

ERNIE: Yes, appoint judges.

JUDGE: Where did you hear this rumor?

ERNIE: From the governor's office.

JUDGE: Who in the governor's office?

ERNIE: I can't say. But I can tell you that it comes from a highly placed and reliable source.

JUDGE: Changing to a system of appointed judges couldn't be done without a constitutional amendment.

ERNIE: Exactly.

JUDGE: Who in the world would support such a crazy idea and why?

ERNIE: Why? Why? Why? Well, supposedly the justification would be to reduce the political influence on existing judges.

JUDGE: Oh sure. And appointing judges would do that? Just look at the Supreme Court. Those judges are appointed and that's about as political a process as anything can get.

ERNIE: As to who is supporting this crazy initiative, I heard it was being pushed by Edwin Greer, a state representative from Northern Louisiana.

JUDGE: Edwin? Representative Edwin Greer?

ERNIE: The same. And I hear that he is even supporting your competitor for the upcoming election.

JUDGE: You're kidding.

ERNIE: No. I'm not kidding.

JUDGE: (*Examines the check very closely.*) This is a substantial contribution.

ERNIE: And there's more where that comes from, a lot more.

JUDGE: I wish I could believe it came without strings, but I know better. There's no such thing as a free lunch. *(Looks at ERNIE.)* What do you expect in return?

ERNIE: Nothing, Judge. Nothing at all. Just continue to demonstrate your fine judicial expertise. (*Pauses.*) By the way, that kook Representative Edwin has been talking about making contingency fees illegal as well.

JUDGE: (*Laughs.*) Wow! That would upset a few apple carts, wouldn't it?

ERNIE: It's ridiculous, of course.

JUDGE: How would you make a living? Isn't that your bread and butter, contingency fees?

ERNIE: Bread and butter and meat and gravy, too. (*Pauses.*) But seriously, how would the poor people get justice without contingency fees? Only the rich could afford justice under that sort of system. Don't you agree?

JUDGE: The rich? Well, perhaps we could have a more developed system of pro-bono work to help with the poorer clients? Or maybe public attorneys appointed by the state? It might work.

ERNIE: Of course it wouldn't work! Think of the indigent schmucks that take bad medications or eat bad food or use bad products. Think of all those poor, injured people. How would they be compensated?

JUDGE: You know as well as I do that only a few lawyers make any real money off those big class action suits.

ERNIE: So? So what if it's true? We still get bad products off the market.

JUDGE: And shut down good companies.

ERNIE: So? If they produce killer products and put profits before people, they deserve to be shut down.

JUDGE: Until there's no one left to sue except those multi-nationals with very different views of accountability and offshore accounts.

ERNIE: Why, to listen to you, Judge, I just might think you support some of these crazy notions.

JUDGE: They might be worth a try. Think of it, you eliminate contingency fees and you take the profit motive out of litigation. It might just make the whole society cheaper. It might unblock the courts from the deluge of litigation. It might be worth exploring.

ERNIE: (*Seriously.*) No worse than say. . .appointed judgeships. That might upset some other apple carts, *n'est-ce pas*? (*Studies the JUDGE.*) And that's not all, Your Honor. There is something even worse.

JUDGE: Worse?

ERNIE: Yes. Representative Edwin supports a movement to place all product liability and malpractice cases before a special commission of only appointed judges.

JUDGE: No jury?

ERNIE: No. No jury at all. Can you imagine such an undemocratic thing? Why it flies in the face of everything sacred in our beloved Constitution.

JUDGE: (*Sits back in his chair.*) They do use the system of appointed judges for malpractice cases in some countries. The say it reduces the passion in the courtroom from uninformed jurors. They're called health courts. Quite a few countries use them.

ERNIE: Communist countries, I suppose.

JUDGE: No, some normal Western European countries, too. The system tends to decrease the number of cases and the awards, especially for pain and suffering. It works overseas pretty well from what I've read.

ERNIE: Wow, then it's a good thing we're in America, don't you agree? (*Approaches the JUDGE.*) Good thing we are in the US of A with the best judicial system in the world with prosperity and justice for all. Don't you agree, Your Honor?

JUDGE: (*Hesitates a bit.*) Of course. Of course.

ERNIE: It would be very disturbing if you supported any of those un-American ideas. I'm sure glad we both agree on some elementary principles of justice.

JUDGE: You know, Ernie, a very wise senior judge once told me that our judicial system was not the best in the world, only the most expensive. He also said our system of justice was not about justice at all, only about settlement.

ERNIE: (*Laughs.*) What a strange idea. (*Pulls out his checkbook.*) By the way, there's plenty more where that comes from. We know how darn expensive these re-election campaigns can get. You get my drift?

JUDGE: (*Winks.*) Of course. I get your drift. And you're right, it's a good thing we live in the US of A, with prosperity and justice for all. . .or at least as long as the money lasts.

(*ERNIE and JUDGE laugh as lights dim to dark.*)

THE END

SETTING UP THE NATIVITY

CAST OF CHARACTERS

BERNADETTE: Woman of distant Italian ancestry. Vivacious, articulate, very animated. She uses her hands when she speaks.

SUZANNA: Older woman of Armenian origin, more recent. She speaks with a slight accent.

CHARLOTTE: American, abrasive and aggressive.

SETTING

The three women are seated behind a folding table. On the table is a nativity set, facing the audience. There is a manger and a few figures are already set up. The women are reaching into plastic boxes and pulling out additional figures, which they unwrap one by one. Then they come around in front to place the figures in the nativity. The figurines are *"santons"* (little saints), typical of Southern France (the region of Provence).

CHARLOTTE: Whose brilliant idea was this anyway?

BERNADETTE: Mine. I thought it would be nice to have a show of nativities from around the world. People like that sort of thing. And I hope it raises quite a bit of money.

CHARLOTTE: I still liked my idea of a Christmas pageant. You put in a bunch of kids on stage and that really attracts all those families. Grandmothers, aunts, uncles, cousins. Everyone comes when there's a bunch of little kids in elf suits singing "I wish you a Merry Christmas." A crowd pleaser translates into more money, pure and simple. That's what a fund raiser is all about, isn't it? More money for the battered women's shelter? (*Continues to unwrap a figure.*) Just wait and see, this project will be a big flop. Who the heck wants to come and see a bunch of nativity sets?

SUZANNA: (*Examines one of the figures and goes to put in the nativity scene.*) I think these little figurines are charming. Each one is different. I think they are beautiful. They remind me of a village scene.

CHARLOTTE: Why so many of them? It's a bit obsessional, isn't it?

BERNADETTE: (*Holds one up and takes it over to the nativity.*) Suzanna, you're right. Each figure represents a different villager and his or her job. There's a baker, a flower seller, a washerwoman, a blacksmith, a priest, a fisherman and lots more. (*Picks up a Virgin Mary.*) And then there are the classical nativity figures like Mary, of course. (*Places the figure at the heart of the nativity and returns to her seat.*) They're all hand painted and each one is different, just like real people.

CHARLOTTE: It this some sort of Italian thing? (*Goes around the table and places a figure at the nativity and returns to her seat.*)

BERNADETTE: (*Continues to unwrap another figure.*) It's really from Southern France in the region of Provence, but it's also done in the Northern part of Italy along the coast near the French Riviera.

CHARLOTTE: We went there couple of years ago. Over-rated if you ask me. The beach, if you can call it that, was made of big pebbles. The women exposed their breasts for every passerby. And a cup of coffee cost seven dollars if you could get one of those snooty French waiters to even serve you.

SUZANNA A wise man. (*Examines it more closely.*) I think it is Melchior.

CHARLOTTE: How do you know?

SUZANNA: Because he's black.

CHARLOTTE: Black. Of course. I guess they were politically correct even back in those days. It never hurts to throw it a bit of color when it comes to marketing. (*Goes over and places a figure.*)

BERNADETTE: I doubt whether they thought about marketing back then.

CHARLOTTE: How the heck do you know?

BERNADETTE: Because St. Francis was supposed to have invented the first nativity set. I read it in a book about *Santons*, and I doubt whether St. Francis was being politically correct way back then.

CHARLOTTE: You read books about little nativity figures?

BERNADETTE: Yes, among other things. I try to read at least three books a month, usually novels, but sometimes non-fiction.

CHARLOTTE: It must be nice to be able to read with all that free time you have since you're not working.

BERNADETTE: (*Clutches her santon in her hand.*) Not working? Don't say that. I take care of my husband, three kids, two dogs, the yard, the pool, the cleaning, the cooking, plus I help entertain an endless stream of guests. I volunteer on least two charitable boards, including this one. Please don't tell me I'm not working!

CHARLOTTE: Oh yeah. Sure. With a rich husband, you can devote your life to culture and charity, and then reap the adulation of a grateful community. I get the picture, St. Bernadette of Fulton, complete with a holier-than-thou attitude. It all makes perfect sense to me.

BERNADETTE: (*Stands up and goes around and places the figurine as she addresses CHARLOTTE.*) What are you talking about? I do a lot for this town. And if you think I have a holier-than-thou attitude, you're completely mistaken. You're the one suffering from an inferiority complex. I don't know why and I don't really care. But you're the one with the problem, not me. (*Waving her hands around in a very Italian manner as she speaks.*)

CHARLOTTE: (*Stands and confronts BERNADETTE with the nativity in between.*) Get your hands out of my face!

BERNADETTE: (*Looks at her own hands in surprise.*) What are you talking about?

CHARLOTTE: Stop shoving your hands in my face. You're invading my private space and I don't appreciate it. It's aggressive.

BERNADETTE: I talk with my hands. (*Drops her hands to her sides.*) It's an Italian thing. (*Looks at her hands.*) Besides, I thought you prided yourself on your cultural sensitivity, your high level of cultural competence.

CHARLOTTE: I have a real culture. I'm American. And I don't hide behind some fake ethnic heritage I picked up living overseas. I've also been around enough to recognize the difference between expressing culture and aggressive personal behavior.

SUZANNA: For heaven's sake! Please stop this, both of you.

BERNADETTE: (*Speaks to SUZANNA.*) She started it. I don't know what it is or why, but there's something about me that irritates her.

SUZANNA: Maybe so, but we're here to set up a nativity for a fund raiser. How do you think it looks to be squabbling when we're here to do something good?

BERNADETTE: Charlotte is attacking me for no reason, and it's not the first time. It's just bullying. (*Makes an imploring gesture to SUZANNA.*) How on earth can you condone that?

SUZANNA: I don't condone it.

BERNADETTE: Then you should condemn it. You of all people should defend me against this sort of thing.

CHARLOTTE: (*Resumes her seat and unwraps another figure.*) What's that supposed to mean?

BERNADETTE: (*Speaks to CHARLOTTE.*) Suzanna's an Armenian, in case you didn't know. Her ancestors were slaughtered by the Turks. One and a half million Armenians were massacred while the world stood by and did nothing.

CHARLOTTE: I'm not slaughtering anyone. I'm just bringing you down to earth where you belong.

BERNADETTE: (*Speaks to CHARLOTTE.*) Not down to earth, down to the slime where people attack others without reason and justify their actions by some misguided sense of social justice.

CHARLOTTE: (*Jumps up off her seat while still clutching a figure.*) Yes! It is long overdue justice for those who have everything: money, power, privilege, and fame. You have it all, Bernadette, and the worse thing is that it seems so effortless, so natural.

BERNADETTE: (*Speaks to CHARLOTTE.*) So you think no one is furnishing any effort?

CHARLOTTE: Sure, someone does, your husband, of course. He's the slave. He's the one up allows all your good deeds as you wander around like an antebellum angel distributing alms to the poor. (*Shakes her head.*)

SUZANNA: Charlotte, please. Don't you think you've said enough?

CHARLOTTE: (*Speaks to SUZANNA.*) It's true. I swear to God. (*Points to BERNADETTE.*) And her sanctimonious attitude is suffocating. I can't breathe around her. Everything she says, everything she does irritates me. She's a wanabe Southern Belle who has assimilated everything rotten about this place and nothing that's good.

BERNADETTE: (*To CHARLOTTE.*) You're crazy! (*Swings her hands in the air.*)

CHARLOTTE: Watch the hands! (*Backs up.*) Is this where you whip out your lash and being flogging the poor, ungrateful deranged slaves?

BERNADETTE: Italians never owned slaves.

SUZANNA: (*Coaxes BERNADETTE, who continues to look astonished, back to her chair.*) Please sit down. We have work to do and this is not helpful. I cannot stand to see this bickering.

(*All three women take their chairs and begin unwrapping characters. There is an awkward silence.*)

BERNADETTE: (*Turns to SUZANNA.*) Suzanna, your people suffered so much. Why don't you say something to Charlotte about her attacks? (*Silence follows.*) It's like those Turks who watched as the Armenians were slaughtered. Or the Germans, or Czechs, or Hungarians who did nothing as their Jewish neighbors were shipped away.

SUZANNA: I try and stay out of conflicts.

BERNADETTE: So did all those other people.

CHARLOTTE: (*Speaks to BERNADETTE.*) So now I'm a Fascist? An arrogant, bullying Fascist? (*No one answers.*) Oh, come on. Say it! If that's what you think, then just come out and say it!

BERNADETTE: You said it. Not me.

CHARLOTTE: That's what you think, isn't it?

BERNADETTE: (*Turns to SUZANNA.*) For heaven's sake Suzanna, speak up for me. You have the ability. And you have the right. You're just as much a citizen here as either of us.

SUZANNA: I am still a guest here.

BERNADETTE: A guest? You were born and raised in America. Since when are you a guest?

SUZANNA: We Armenians always kept a low profile. It is better that way. The less people notice you, the less likely they will be jealous of your success. Jealousy breeds hatred.

CHARLOTTE: Hatred, jealousy, aggression, injustice! All these big words, spilling down from the throne of your moral superiority. You are both something else.

SUZANNA: Charlotte, I beg of you. Everyone has suffered from some indignities, from some frustrations, from some injustices. But does that give us the right to inflict that same treatment on the innocent people around us?

CHARLOTTE: Yes, it does. And the closer the so-called innocent target, the better.

BERNADETTE: (*Speaks to CHARLOTTE.*) That's it! (*Sighs and shakes her head.*) This conversation is over. Every time you want to be cruel, just give me some warning and I'll stop listening. I may be forgiving, but I'm not a masochist.

CHARLOTTE: And I'm not a sadist!

SUZANNA: That is enough. Stop it now! We have work to do. (*Speaks to CHARLOTTE.*) It doesn't matter what any of us thinks about the others. All that matters is that we behave like civilized women. This is ridiculous. We are grown women, not little girls on a playground. (*Points to the nativity.*) Let us finish up with the work here. (*Sits down and the three women continue to work.)* This is a community project that reflects on all of us. This is for battered women. Let us try and remember that. This is also the season for peace on earth, good will to men. . .and women. Or did I miss something? (*Holds up another figure.*) Another wise man. How appropriate.

CHARLOTTE: (*Stands up and tosses the figurine she is holding back into the box.*) That's it! I have had it up to here with sanctimonious do gooders. I get enough lectures in church every Sunday and I sure as hell don't have to listen to them from you two.

BERNADETTE: You don't need to use profanity. It just reflects an immature mind.

CHARLOTTE: (*Grabs a sweater or a jacket.*) I'm outta here. (*Yells at BERNADETTE.*) And don't think I'm not going to try and get you thrown out of this organization. I was here before you came and I'll be here after you're expelled.

BERNADETTE: You can't do that.

CHARLOTTE: You bet your sweet intellectual ass that I can. (*Stomps off the stage.*)

BERNADETTE: (*Speaks to SUZANNA.*) Why didn't you say something? Why didn't you defend me?

SUZANNA: I told you I avoid conflict. Besides, Charlotte may be unpleasant, but she is powerful and she has powerful friends. Sometimes survival is more important than confrontation.

BERNADETTE: (*Sets her figurine on the table.*) I can't believe you're saying that. Survival is never worth capitulation.

SUZANNA: Sometimes capitulation is the only road to survival. I will not even tell you what my grandparents had to do to get out of Turkey.

BERNADETTE: Then don't tell me. I don't want to hear. I don't understand not being able to defend a friend under attack. Why don't you finish up here alone? I'm too upset to finish.

(BERNADETTE *picks up a sweater and leaves the stage in the opposite direction from CHARLOTTE. There is a long pause. SUZANNA goes back to work.*)

SUZANNA: And here's Joseph. (*Goes and puts the figure in the nativity. Then she goes back and unwraps the figure that BERNADETTE left on the table.*) And last but not least, here's the baby Jesus. (*Places the baby in the manger.*)

(*SUZANNA stands alone in front and admires the nativity and stares at it in silence before walking slowly off stage. SUZANNA's posture is a little stooped. After SUZANNA leaves the stage, a single spotlight shines on the nativity. The lights dim to black.*)

THE END

SIGNING THE OATH

CAST OF CHARACTERS

PRESIDENT BOOTH: President of Fairfield Christian College. He is dressed in a suit and tie, with or without a sport jacket.

PROFESSOR TERRY HARTFORD: Teacher at Fairfield Christian College. He is more casually dressed, perhaps in a sweater and slacks with loafers.

SETTING

This is the president's office. There is a desk and a couple of chairs. There can be a bookshelf and some books. There is an embroidered piece of art with the words "I am the Way, the Truth, and the Light."

BOOTH: (*Holds a big bunch of papers in HARTFORD's direction.*) Hartford, I want you to sign this loyalty oath. You are only one of a handful of holdouts and I can't wait much longer.

HARTFORD: President Booth, I haven't made up my mind yet. It's a complex decision.

BOOTH: What's so complex about it? The issues are straightforward. You either want to be part of our Christ-centered university team or you don't.

HARTFORD: With all due respect, I believe that's a bit simplistic. There are several men and women of great intelligence and virtue who have chosen not to sign this document. Roberts in History, Dufour in Creative Writing, Jones in Music. I admire those people greatly.

BOOTH: And you do not admire me, or your other fine colleagues who have already signed?

HARTFORD: I do respect and admire some of those who have signed. Not all. But that's not the point. It's a question of personal conscience.

BOOTH: Yes, of course. Personal conscience. (*Pauses.*) Listen Hartford, may I call you Terry?

HARTFORD: It seems a little late to be cultivating such intimacy, but whatever you prefer.

BOOTH: Terry, I admire your work, your dedication. I think you have achieved great things at this school over the last decade, but, quite frankly, no one is irreplaceable.

HARTFORD: I understand you could replace me in a heartbeat. Good people in Nineteenth Century English literature are a dime a dozen.

BOOTH: Yes, they are. But you have the virtue of being a long-time presence, a known entity in the academic and general community. Besides, you have developed a certain following among the student body. Let's face it, you're popular and you're an asset for the institution and I would much rather keep you than replace you.

HARTFORD: Thank you for the compliment. I wish I could return it, but quite frankly, you have brought a lot of controversy to this school, especially with your dismissal of Dr. Bernstein. That was interpreted as an anti-Semitic gesture by just about everyone on and off campus.

BOOTH: That is unfair and you know it. Bernstein did not share our religious vision for this institution as clearly defined by the Board of Regents. Sharing that vision is the least we can expect from the faculty in a school of our affiliation, don't you agree?

HARTFORD: So that means no agnostics, no Catholics, no Buddhists, no Muslims, no blacks, and no homosexuals at Fairfield Christian College? Is that your vision of the perfect faculty? How do you hope to create a broader world vision among our sheltered students like that? A white Protestant faculty, is that it? Is that your vision of diversity?

BOOTH: That is untrue and unfair. Besides, if what you say is true, why do you think I want you to stay?

HARTFORD: What exactly are you implying?

BOOTH: I'm not implying anything. (*Pauses.*) Some students and faculty have reported that you are less than enthusiastic about church attendance.

HARTFORD: And?

BOOTH: And that being unmarried, your views on the sanctity of marriage may be less than orthodox.

HARTFORD: So you consider me a homosexual agnostic? Is that what you think I am?

BOOTH: Please. I'm not here to discuss your private life, but your academic qualifications and achievements. We don't want everyone to think and look alike, do we?

HARTFORD: You could have fooled me. From what I can tell, you want the faculty and the students to all look alike.

BOOTH: That's unfair and untrue. We embrace diversity, as long as it remains within the boundaries of our Christ-centered vision of education.

HARTFORD: Right. I'm not really sure it is useful to discuss this. What exactly do you want from me? Why is it so important for me to sign this document?

BOOTH: Aren't you related to Senator Harry Hartford?

HARTFORD: Yes. That's my great-uncle.

BOOTH: Let's be frank. (*Puts his arm around HARTFORD, who pulls away.*) I'm willing to overlook some of your personal idiosyncrasies and indiscretions in return for some help. There is some school funding legislation before the state senate which will greatly impact the future of Fairfield College.

HARTFORD: You want me to influence my great-uncle to get some crummy law passed?

BOOTH: Precisely. And I would hardly call this a "crummy law." It has huge implications for all private schools in this state. We need to ensure its passage, regardless of the means.

HARTFORD: That doesn't sound very compatible with our spiritual mission statement.

BOOTH: (*Moves away from HARTFORD.*) Spirituality must take a back seat to practicality where finances are concerned.

HARTFORD: Is this part of our Christ-centered vision? Sell out our moral values to the legislators in return for a handful of silver?

BOOTH: That's a snide remark, which I will overlook because thirty million dollars is not a handful of silver. In this era of budgetary restrictions, it may well mean the difference between keeping this school open or not. We have had some disgruntled traditional donors and a drop in enrollment. Both have negatively impacted the bottom line. We need that legislation passed. We need that infusion of state funds, at least to get us through this current fiscal crisis.

HARTFORD: Ah. I see. No educational mission without a profit margin.

BOOTH: Precisely.

HARTFORD: Doesn't tampering with the legislature make you feel a little morally compromised?

BOOTH: No. We do what we must for the good of Fairfield College. And I would like you to do the same, for the good of this institution.

HARTFORD: The institution? Isn't that just another way of saying you want me to do this for you personally?

BOOTH: No. I'm not the beneficiary. The school is the beneficiary. That seems clear to me.

HARTFORD: But with no school, there's no president, is there? So isn't this really just a personal request for your personal benefit?

BOOTH: What do you what me to say? Of course I will benefit directly, but that is not the point. The survival of the school is at stake here and I will not be its last president, regardless of what unsavory tactics I need to employ to achieve that goal. If it makes it any easier on you, then I will ask you to do this for me as a personal favor. And if not out of respect, then I'm asking you to do it for friendship's sake.

HARTFORD: For friendship's sake, eh?

BOOTH: Exactly. So please go ahead and sign this oath.

HARTFORD: (*Takes the document and leafs through it.*) Doesn't this thing say that I can't drink, swear or show excessive displays of physical affection in public?

BOOTH: Yes, it does.

HARTFORD: What about dancing?

BOOTH: Dancing is negotiable. Besides, I hear you are an excellent dancer and it would be a pity to deprive the community of such a well rounded academician.

HARTFORD: I don't know, Mr. President. Allowing dancing smacks of moral degeneration.

BOOTH: On the contrary, it's merely a reflection of my admiration for you as a person as well as testimony to the long-term relationship between ourselves and our families. Our friendship goes back decades and our family relationships go back even more. Who knows? Perhaps we're related? You could be one of my long-lost cousins.

HARTFORD: Long friendship? What are you talking about? We haven't exchanged more than twenty words in the last ten years. And I'm not sure I want to be related to you. (*Hands the papers back to BOOTH.*) Here, take your loyalty oath.

BOOTH: But we are part of the same family, Terry, whether you like it our not. We are brothers in Christ.

HARTFORD: Yes. I suppose we are brothers in Christ. And now I am saying goodbye, brother. Or perhaps I should say goodbye, cousin?

BOOTH: You'll regret it, Hartford! You still have to live in this community. I can be charitable, but I can also summon up the wrath of God against you and your ungodly ways. I can make this town a living hell for you.

HARTFORD: First the carrot, then the stick, eh? (*Shakes his head in disgust.*) No, I won't regret it. I don't have to stay here. It would be an inconvenience to leave, that's all. No, I won't sign your loyalty oath. I just hope this school survives all this turmoil and goes on to better days. And I hope you will have the moral integrity to accept some of the responsibility for those disgruntled donors and frightened parents. We're all either part of the solution or part of the problem.

BOOTH: I'm sorry you won't be part of the solution with us. And Fairfield Christian College will not only survive, but it will prosper with or without you or me. I believe in this place. I believe in the sanctity of our educational mission. I am not the evil or ignorant person you may think I am. I do regret we could not reach some sort of an agreement.

HARTFORD: But we have, President Booth. We have agreed to disagree. And now I need to be going. My résumé needs some refreshing. Goodbye and good luck.

(*HARTFORD extends his hand and BOOTH extends his. The loyalty oath accidently falls to the ground with a plop. HARTFORD bends to pick it up, but BOOTH stops him from bending down and pulls him back up.*)

BOOTH: Leave it alone. I'll pick it up after you leave. I'm truly sorry to see you go. I admire you as a teacher and a human being. But we each have to live in accordance with our own conscience. And we both have to do what we feel is necessary to accomplish God's will. Christ be with you.

HARTFORD: And also with you. (*Pauses.*) I'll talk to my great-uncle about the legislation. He's pretty old and set in his ways. Plus he may not be too concerned if there's nothing in it for him. Anyway, I'll do what I can and he usually values my input. I don't want to see this place close any more than you do. That would be a great tragedy.

(*HARTFORD turns and walks away. The loyalty oath lies on the ground. Lights dim to dark.*)

THE END

TWENTY DEAD, MORE WOUNDED

CAST OF CHARACTERS

MR. MILLER: President of the university.

MR. NORRIS: Vice President of the university.

MR. O'REILLY: Security Officer of the university.

MR. PORTER: Plaintiff's attorney.

SETTING

There are three chairs grouped together and one, the "witness stand," placed apart. The audience is the jury.

(*University PRESIDENT MILLER is in the front center of the stage, bathed in a pool of light. The others are in the background.*)

PRESIDENT: That was by far the worst day of my life. Twenty dead, as many wounded: professors, students, visitors, security personnel, and even someone's baby. (*Pauses.*) All that because some crazy guy wanted to make a name for himself. And then there was the memorial service and the funeral, and the recriminations about inadequate security. (*Pauses.*) Inadequate security. How do you defend against a lunatic with an assault rifle? How do you cope with a catastrophe? We're supposed to be dealing with learning, libraries, books and on-line courses, not assault rifles. For heaven's sake, the guy wasn't even a student. And just when things appeared to calm down among the students, faculty and general public, the lawyers began. Who was responsible? Who was to blame? How much should it cost? Who pays the price?

(*The lights come up. VICE PRESIDENT NORRIS and SECURITY OFFICER O'REILLY come on stage to join PRESIDENT MILLER. They help set up four chairs. Three are for them and one is off to the side, a witness stand. ATTORNEY*

PORTER comes on stage. O'Reilly takes the "witness stand," the chair off to the side.)

PORTER: Ladies and gentlemen of the jury (*Speaks to the audience/ jury.*) Mr. O'Reilly was responsible for the so-called security on the campus. What security? What kind of security would allow twenty innocent people to be shot to death and twenty more to be maimed before someone from the SWAT team killed the perpetrator? (*Turns to O'REILLY.*) Were you the Chief Security Officer at the university at the time of the shooting?

O'REILLY: Yes.

PORTER: And how is it that a heavily armed killer could wander onto the campus and kill twenty innocent people?

O'REILLY: The campus is not a prison or an armed fortress.

PORTER: No metal detectors?

O'REILLY: No.

PORTER: No security check points?

O'REILLY: No, sir.

PORTER: No student notification system?

O'REILLY: Not at that time.

PORTER: Not at that time? (*To the audience/jury.*) I'm sure that's a great consolation to the twenty dead, twenty wounded, and the hundred of grieving family members and friends.

O'REILLY: Those systems were not common on most campuses at that time.

PORTER: But they did exist, did they not?

O'REILLY: At some campuses in the United States, yes, they did exist, especially in larger, more dangerous urban areas.

PORTER: Well, apparently we are more dangerous here than you thought.

O'REILLY: Is that a question?

PORTER: (*Ignores O'REILLY.*) Isn't it the responsibility of a security officer to provide security?

O'REILLY: Yes, in the limits of our resources.

PORTER: And were those resources available to you at that time?

O'REILLY: No.

PORTER: Thank you. That's all. The witness may step down.

(*O'REILLY leaves the witness stand and returns to his chair with the others.*)

PORTER: I call Vice President Norris.

(VICE PRESIDENT NORRIS *takes the witness stand.*)

PORTER: State you name for the jury.

VICE PRESIDENT: Mr. George Norris

PORTER: And were you Vice President of the university at the time of the shooting?

VICE PRESIDENT: Yes.

PORTER: Was one of your assigned duties to oversee Mr. O'Reilly's Security Office?

VICE PRESIDENT: Yes.

PORTER: And why exactly did you not provide an early notification system, security checks, metal detectors, and adequate man power to prevent the horrible tragedy which occurred at your campus?

VICE PRESIDENT: We did not have the resources available at that time and such a atrocious attack was considered highly unlikely.

PORTER: Unlikely?

VICE PRESIDENT: Yes, highly unlikely.

PORTER: But not impossible, as events clearly proved.

VICE PRESIDENT: No, not impossible.

PORTER: In fact, had you not discussed just such a possibility after the Columbine Massacre at your Executive Committee meeting in the proceeding October. (*Flourishes some papers.*)

VICE PRESIDENT: Yes, we did discuss it.

PORTER: And what did the Executive Committee decide?

VICE PRESIDENT: We decided that it would not be cost effective to install metal detectors, additional check points or a student notification system at that time.

PORTER: So you decided to save some money and it resulted in the avoidable death of 20 people, plus 20 more maimed, and hundreds affected for the rest of their lives.

VICE PRESIDENT: We did not allocate the resources for additional security at that time.

PORTER: But those same meeting minutes reveal that you did allocate some $250,000 for the University Art Museum, is that correct?

VICE PRESIDENT: Yes.

PORTER: (*Addresses the audience/jury.*) So your Executive Committee decided to spend money on art rather than on security for the student body, is that true?

    (*VICE PRESIDENT remains silent.*)

PORTER: (*Yells at the top of his voice.*) Is that true?

VICE PRESIDENT: I guess you could look at it that way.

PORTER: (*Again he addresses the audience/jury.*) Is there any other way to look at it? (*Pauses and turns back to VICE PRESIDENT NORRIS.*) Could additional security resources at that time have prevented this tragedy, Mr. Norris?

VICE PRESIDENT: It's not at all clear. The assailant came in through the student housing and made his way to the engineering building. He went through the emergency exit. Those are places where we would normally not place a metal detector or security guard.

PORTER: Normally not? (*Pauses.*) So what is normal about a crazed gunman coming in and destroying the lives of hundreds of people directly and indirectly?

VICE PRESIDENT: There is nothing normal about any of it. There is nothing normal about an unstable individual buying assault weapons and ammunition without undergoing a decent background check either.

PORTER: You mean you oppose our constitutionally protected right to bear arms?

VICE PRESIDENT: I favor restrictions.

PORTER: (*Addresses the audience/jury.*) I think we understand your priorities: money over safety, art over safety, and restrictions on constitutional rights rather than assuming your responsibilities. (*Pauses.*) That will be all, Mr. Norris. I call President Miller to the stand.

> (*VICE PRESIDENT NORRIS takes his seat and PRESIDENT MILLER comes and sits in the witness chair.*)

PORTER: Please state your name and position.

PRESIDENT: My name is Charles Miller and I was President of the university at the time of the shooting.

PORTER: Was it not your responsibility to oversee all aspects of campus life?

PRESIDENT: Yes.

PORTER: Did that include overseeing Vice President Norris and, by extension, the Security Department under Mr. O'Reilly?

PRESIDENT: Yes.

PORTER: As President of the university, were you not the Chairman of the Executive Committee as well?

PRESIDENT: Yes.

PORTER: Mr. Miller, why did you leave your position of President of the university after the shooting?

PRESIDENT: I felt my presence was a distraction from the healing process of the university.

PORTER: Healing process?

PRESIDENT: The University Board encouraged my departure in the best interest of the university.

PORTER: They fired you, did they not?

PRESIDENT: No. They offered me a severance package and encouraged me to leave.

PORTER: They fired you.

PRESIDENT: No. I chose to leave.

PORTER: Yes, you chose to leave, just like you refused to leave your office and go to the emergency operations center on the day of the tragedy. Is that correct?

PRESIDENT: The situations are different, but on the day of the shooting, I felt that my place was at the university during its hour of crisis and not at the emergency operations center.

PORTER: Retrospectively, the Board did not agree.

PRESIDENT: You will have to ask the board members about that.

PORTER: Of course. (*Pauses.*) But you were president at the time of the Executive Committee meeting when a decision was made not to allocate additional funds to campus security.

PRESIDENT: Yes. That is correct.

PORTER: So you agreed that the University Art Museum was worth more than the lives of the students.

PRESIDENT: That was not the choice.

PORTER: But that turned out to be the reality, did it not?

PRESIDENT: A terrible tragedy occurred on our campus, which devastated the lives of hundreds of people. My heart goes out to each and every one of those people now and at that time.

PORTER: Your heart? (*Addresses the audience/jury.*) Those people don't need your heart, they need justice! They need indemnification! They need money to live, to put their lives back together and to go about their business.

PRESIDENT: It's all about the money isn't it?

PORTER: No. It's about safety. It's about justice. It's about your dereliction of duty and your abandonment of your responsibilities in an hour of crisis.

PRESIDENT: I used my best judgment at the time.

PORTER: Your best judgment was not enough. (*To the audience/ jury*) And I implore you of the jury to send the strangest possible message to this man, and the university he represented, and to the heartless insurance company that covers them all, that their actions were unacceptable. And that their actions continue to be unacceptable. (*Addresses PRESIDENT MILLER.*) You voted for an art museum instead of for increased student security, for God's sake. (*Addresses the audience/ jury.*) Mr. Miller says it's about money, but I say it is about justice. This was an avoidable tragedy!

PRESIDENT: And this is, too.

PORTER: (*Spins around to address PRESIDENT MILLER.*) What did you say?

PRESIDENT: I said that this is, too.

PORTER: Ladies and gentlemen of the jury, this is the height of arrogance. Mr. Norris challenges our right to bear arms and Mr. Miller here challenges our right to seek redress of our grievances in the courts. Is that what you are saying Ex-President Miller?

PRESIDENT: I am saying that the shooting was a senseless tragedy and compounding that tragedy in court is more of the same, senseless tragedy.

PORTER: (*Looks at the audience/jury.*) I am stunned. Ladies and gentlemen of the jury, send a message to these monsters. (*Points at the defendants.*) Let them hear the voice of God-fearing righteous Americans, untainted by liberal prejudices. Let them hear you loud and clear. We have a right to bear arms. We have a right to send our children to school and expect them to be safe and sound. And God and the Constitution of the United States give us the right and obligation to seek redress for grievances in court when those expectations are not satisfied. (*Pauses.*) Don't do this for me. I am a humble player in this terrible drama. Do it for the dead, the wounded, and the heartbroken. Send an unequivocal message to these evil and arrogant men that we seek justice and we will have it!

(*PRESIDENT steps forward. He is in a pool of light and the others are in darkness. He addresses the audience.*)

PRESIDENT: You can guess the outcome. (*Motions to O'REILLY.*) Security Officer O'Reilly went to work for the local mall. A few years later, he took early retirement. (*Motions to VICE PRESIDENT NORRIS.*) Vice President Norris got out of academics and became a security consultant for a company selling student notification systems. (*Pauses.*) I followed the board's advice and took a severance package. Every single day, I think about the victims. My heart still goes out to each and every one of them. The insurance company paid out a lot of money. The insurance premium for our university, and all other universities for that matter, tripled. The university closed the art museum and the theater program, and the high school outreach program as well. They fired about 15 adjunct professors and increased class sizes. They also cut out a number of un-endowed scholarships. (*Pauses.*) But they did install a student notification system, metal detectors in the dorms and classrooms, and they installed security check points at all the entrances. (*Pauses.*) And Mr. Porter sent his entire staff off on a week long Caribbean cruise to celebrate their great triumph. I heard he bought a beach house at Gulf Shores, and a mansion on a golf course somewhere. He expanded his staff by a bunch of attorneys and a pack of paralegals and he advertises regularly on television. I hear he's even going into politics. (*Pauses.*) I got rid of my hunting rifle and my hand gun. I couldn't stand the sight of them. Plus, my wife was afraid I might commit suicide because of depression. (*Pauses.*) And I still might.

(*Lights out.*)

THE END

A LA LOUISIANE!

(FRENCH CORRECTIONS BY
DR. CHANTAL MATON AND MARGOT MILLER)

CAST OF CHARACTERS

PIERRE: Young married man, descendent of original French settlers, speaks English with a marked French accent.

CATHERINE: Pierre's wife and also from an original French family speaks English with a marked French accent.

JOHN: Young married man of American immigration, fluent in French but speaks it with a marked American accent.

MARY: John's wife and also an American, who speaks fluent French, but also with a marked, but not unpleasant, American accent

AUTHOR'S NOTE

Two couples, one Creole (French, born in the colony) and one American, bilingual French and English and living in Louisiana, meet on three important dates in Louisiana history: 1803 just prior to the sale of Louisiana by Napoleon, 1815 at the Battle of New Orleans, and 1832 at the twentieth anniversary of Louisiana statehood. To reflect the linguistic changes during that period, the first act is in French, the second French and English, and the third in English only.

ACT I (La Nouvelle Orléans/New Orleans, 1803)

Les quatre personnes sont assises autour d'une table élégante. CATHERINE et PIERRE sont les hôtes et MARY et JOHN sont leurs invités. Tout le monde parle en français, mais MARY et JOHN parlent avec un accent américain marqué. La table est richement pourvue, assiettes, verres, plateaux et chandeliers élégants. Ils sont habilles de vêtements d'époque, c'est-à-dire,

1803, année de la vente de la Louisiane aux Etats-Unis par l'Empereur Napoléon.
(The four people are seated around an elegant table. CATHERINE and PIERRE are the hosts and MARY and JOHN are their guests. Everyone speaks in French, but the MARY and JOHN speak with a marked American accent. The table is set with elegant plates, glasses, serving dishes and candle holders. They are dressed in clothing typical of the year 1803, same year that Louisiana was sold to the United States by the Emperor Napoleon.)

PIERRE : (*Il propose un toast. [He proposes a toast.]*) A Notre Empereur bien-aimé, Napoléon Bonaparte! Le nouveau souverain de la Louisiane.

(*Tout le monde lève leurs verres et ils les chiquent les uns avec les autres.[Everyone raises their glass and touches it to the other glasses.]*)

TOUS : A l'Empereur!

JOHN : (*Il parle Français, mais avec un accent très marqué. [He speaks in French, but with a marked accent.]*) Pierre, parlez-moi franchement, croyez-vous que nous ferons partie de la France pour longtemps?

PIERRE : Longtemps? Bien sûr. Mais pourquoi posez-vous une question aussi étrange, mon cher Jean?

JOHN : J'ai entendu une rumeur comme quoi Napoléon veut vendre la Louisiane aux Américains.

CATHERINE : Quel drôle d'idée! Napoléon vient juste de prendre possession de ce pays. Le Préfet Laussat vient à peine d'arriver ici pour former la nouvelle administration. Pourquoi l'Empereur vendrait-il la Louisiane?

JOHN : Pour l'argent, bien sûr. Pourquoi pensez-vous que les gens vendent leurs biens?

CATHERINE : L'argent, l'argent, l'argent! Vous Américains ne pensez qu'à ça. Il y a quand même d'autres choses dans le monde à pars l'argent, n'est-ce pas?

MARY : Catherine, je ne veux pas paraître plus matérialiste que les autres, mais sans argent, il n'y a pas de bonheur, bien que certains philosophes veulent nous le faire croire.

CATHERINE : Tu m'étonnes, Marie. Regarde nous autres. Nous n'avons pas de fortune et portant nous vivons très bien.

JOHN : Pas de fortune? (*A PIERRE.*) Vous avez des problèmes d'argents, Pierre?

PIERRE : Catherine, s'il te plaît. Il ne faut pas inquiéter nos amis en leur donnant les fausses impressions. D'abord, nous avons assez d'argent et ensuite, il ne faut jamais parler d'argent à table. Ça risque d'être considéré comme grossier.

JOHN : Je sais que les discussions d'argent sont mal vues par nous amis Créoles, mais c'est une luxe des aisés de considérer l'argent comme quelque chose de malpropre ou trop basse classe que pour être un sujet de conversation entre amis.

PIERRE : Merci pour ta considération, mais je vous assure que nous sommes dans une situation financière enviable. Et je ne suis pas si détaché de la réalité pour ne pas me rendre compte que sans argent, la vie est difficile. La pauvreté est toujours pénible. Mais notre chère Louisiane a été très généreuse avec nous. Et je trouve que n'importe qui avec un peu d'intelligence et d'efforts peut faire fortune ici. Regardons nous autres. Nous avons commencé comme des marchands démunis et maintenant nous sommes les gros propriétaires avec des plantations et les centaines d'esclaves.

MARY : Et les très jolies plantations, je dois dire.

CATHERINE : En parlant des plantations, vous devez absolument nous rendre visite avant que la saison d'hiver ne s'achève. Il fait insupportable là-bas pendant l'été, mais le printemps et l'automne sont délicieux. Nous bénéficions de la fraîcheur de la rivière.

JOHN : La fraîcheur? Ma chère Catherine, je ne peux guère parler de la fraîcheur de la rivière en la Louisiane. Il fait chaud ici les neuf dixièmes de l'année. De plus, c'est difficile pour moi de quitter mes commerces, peu importe la saison. Nous vendons de plus en plus de marchandises durant toute l'année.

PIERRE : Vendons Achetons. Encore des affaires. Parlons plutôt de cette affaire de la soi-disant vente de la Louisiane. Ca m'intéresse. Par qui as-tu appris ces nouvelles invraisemblables?

JOHN : Par Monsieur La Place, employé chez Monsieur le Préfet Laussat lui-même.

CATHERINE : Ridicule! Je connais ce Monsieur La Place de réputation et je vous assure que ce n'est pas très bonne.

JOHN : Peut-être. Mais pourquoi inventerait-il quelque chose comme ça? Tout le monde sait que l'Empereur a perdu plusieurs milliers de soldats à San Domingue. Comment veux-tu qu'il défende la Louisiane contre les anglais? Il n'a plus de soldats disponibles pour le faire.

CATHERINE : Maudits anglais. Je déteste cette sale race.

MARY : Un peu de charité, Catherine. Après tout, John et moi sommes aussi les anglophones d'origine.

CATHERINE : Bien sûr. Excusez-moi. Mais vous êtes complètement différents.

JOHN : Parce que nous parlons français, peut-être?

CATHERINE : Non. Pas simplement pour cela. Vous êtes aussi très cultivés et sympathiques. Vous comprenez la sensibilité de notre race.

PIERRE : Ma chère Catherine, nous sommes tous de la même race ici, tu ne crois pas?

CATHERINE : Oh, mon Dieu. Je ne voulais pas insinuer que vous venez d'une mélange de races, simplement que vous êtes d'origine anglo-saxonne et nous sommes d'origine gallique. C'est tout.

MARY : J'ai très bien compris. Mais finalement, crois-tu que cette soi-disant différence de race ait tellement d'importance?

CATHERINE : Oui, bien sûr. Enorme. Nous sommes dérivés des Romains, les conquérants de l'Europe, l'Afrique et l'Asie. Et les anglo-saxons sont d'origine barbare.

JOHN : Barbare? Je crois que tu t'aggraves ton cas. Maintenant, Mary et moi sommes simplement les barbares.

CATHERINE : Pas vous autres, bien sûr. Je parle de l'histoire antique. Les Romains avez déjà développé une civilisation remarquable pendant que les gens autour vivaient un mode de vie primitif. Les gallo-romains avaient quelques siècles d'avance sur les autres peuples d'Europe. Et cette avance continue de nos jours.

JOHN : (*JOHN rit. [JOHN laughs].*) Rappelle-toi que les représentants de la race remarquable ont coupé la tête de Louis XVI et Marie Antoinette et beaucoup d'autres.

CATHERINE : Quelques dégâts sont toujours le prix du progrès.

JOHN : M'enfin, Catherine. Je ne savais pas que tu étais une dame si révolutionnaire.

PIERRE : Ma chère épouse a toujours été assez émancipée. Tu n'as pas remarqué avec quelle facilité elle discute de l'actualité aussi bien que du passé lointain?

JOHN : C'est rare parmi les femmes Créoles. Et à quoi doit-elle cette émancipation d'esprit?

CATHERINE : A la lecture, mon cher Jean. Et je ne parle pas simplement de la Bible. Je parle de Voltaire, Molière, Rousseau, Marat, et de notre cher Empereur.

MARY : J'ai toujours admiré tes idées progressistes. Et ton niveau d'instruction. C'est insupportable ces femmes Créoles que ne discutent que de leur toilette et du prochain bal.

CATHERINE : Et moi, j'ai toujours admiré ta sophistication et ouverture d'esprit, Marie. Des traits de caractère bien rares chez mes compatriotes Créoles.

MARY : Et pourquoi ce manque d'intérêt pour le monde de l'esprit chez les femmes Créoles?

PIERRE : Je réponds pour elle. En un mot, la paresse. Et pour ça, j'admire l'esprit d'initiative des américains, femmes et hommes. Ils ont quand même un certain sens pratique, un sens d'organisation.

JOHN : Et avec cette admiration, peut-être seras-tu content si Napoléon vendait la Louisiane au Président Jefferson. Comme ça, vous pourriez tirer parti de cet esprit d'initiative et d'organisation?

PIERRE : A Dieu ne plaise! Nous avons attendus des décennies pour redevenir Français. Et maintenant, grâce à Napoléon, nous le sommes. Je propose un autre toast à l'Empereur!

TOUS : A l'Empereur!

JOHN : Et au Président Jefferson, aussi un américain remarquable, très francophile paraît-il.

TOUS : Au Président Jefferson!

CATHERINE : Et à notre belle amitié, l'amitié franco-américaine!

MARY : Catherine! Les femmes ne proposent pas de toasts.

CATHERINE : Nous habitons la Louisiane. Je crois que les femmes peuvent proposer des toasts. Au moins, à l'amitié. *(Elle soulève son verre de nouveau. [She raises her glass again.])* A l'amitié éternelle.

TOUS : A l'amitié!

PIERRE : Ecoutez. C'est le bruit d'un bal Créole pas loin d'ici.

MARY : Je connais cette musique. C'est une polonaise. Une danse très à la mode à Paris, parait-il.

CATHERINE : Tu les connais, les pas de la danse?

MARY : Pas très bien.

CATHERINE : Tu peux nous les enseigner, ici, maintenant?

JOHN : Non, s'il te plaît. Je danse comme un pied.

PIERRE : Moi aussi. J'ai deux pieds gauches.

MARY ET CATHERINE: Allons-y. Debout. Dansons ensemble.

JOHN ET PIERRE : Non!

MARY : Allez. On essaie. *(Elle tire sur JOHN tandis que CATHERINE entraîne PIERRE. [She pulls JOHN while CATHERINE pulls PIERRE.])*

Eh bien, les mains devant comme ceci. Et on avance. Un-deux-saut, un-deux-saut, six pas courus. Très bien. On répète tout depuis le début.

ACT II (La Nouvelle Orléans/New Orleans, 1815)

L'acte II se passe dans une salle publique avec les bancs en bois. Une ombre par terre suggère peut-être la lumière qui passe par une fenêtre. La scène est très dépouillée. MARY et CATHERINE sont habillées de voiles comme si elles sortaient de l'église. Dans cet acte, chaque personne parle sa langue maternelle.
(Act II takes place in a public room with wooden benches. Perhaps there is a shadow on the ground that suggest light passing through a window. The stage is very stark. MARY and CATHERINE are dressed with veils as if they were leaving a church service. In this act, each person speaks their native tongue.)

CATHERINE: Tu entends les canons?

MARY : Yes.

CATHERINE : Je me demande si Monsieur Lafitte est arrivé à temps avec ses pirates?

MARY: He's a thief and a criminal.

CATHERINE : Oui, bien sûr. Tu as complètement raison. Mais dans les circonstances actuelles, ses armes et ses hommes peuvent faire la différence entre la victoire et la défaite.

MARY: Victory? Defeat? Yes, I suppose you are right. Sometimes we have to temper our moral values for the circumstances. No one wants the English to win. *(Elle écoute. [She listens.])* They sound so close, the guns. You hear the rumbling?

CATHERINE : Comme le tonnerre. Comme l'ouragan.

MARY: This year has been nothing but political hurricanes: war, threats of war, in Europe, in the United States.

CATHERINE : Oui. C'est comme les guerres en Europe n'ont pas assez de place et elles se déplacent dans notre chère Louisiane.

MARY: Yes, our beloved Louisiana that no one wanted, not even your Emperor. He sold you out for 22 million. Not a bad price for an empire.

CATHERINE : Oui. Ton Président Jefferson a fait une affaire au dépens des Français.

MARY: Yes, quite an affair for a territory that no one really wanted. Not the French, not the Spanish, not even the English, really. Just the Americans.

CATHERINE : Oui, bien sûr. Les Américains. Et maintenant ils arrivent ici par milliers chaque jour, comme des cigales, ma chère Marie. Ils dévorent tout. Ils détruisent tout. C'est honteux.

MARY: You are too hard, Catherine. Governor Claiborne has been good to the French speakers. He as always tried to accommodate the Creoles as best he could.

CATHERINE : Il ne parle même pas Français. Il a une horreur des gens de couleur libres et pourtant ces gens se battent à côté des autres contre les anglais. Nous étions trahis par Napoléon, c'est tout.

MARY: Don't you think that's a bit dramatic and unjust. Napoleon had no way of holding onto Louisiana. He could sell it to the Americans or lose it to the British for nothing. Besides, look at your prosperity under the American flag: your home, your plantations, your businesses. You and Pierre are rich and happy.

CATHERINE : Riche, c'est vrai. Heureux, parfois. Et maintenant avec les Britanniques presque assurés de gagner, nous serons de nouveau sur l'emprise des anglais. Regarde ce qu'ils ont fait avec les pauvres Acadiens. Combien de temps faudra-t-il avant qu'ils ne fassent la même chose avec nous? Où irons-nous les Français? Au Mexique? En Afrique? Regarde la triste histoire de ces réfugiés de San Domingue. Ils sont arrives ici sans argent, sans esclaves, sans amis. Ils sont arrivés par milliers et ils étaient acceptés ici, juste comme les Acadiens auparavant. Ils sont devenus les bons citoyens.

MARY : Like the handsome Louis Delaforte by chance?

CATHERINE : Qu'est-ce que tu suggères?

MARY: Pierre must be blind not to see how you look at Louis every time you see him. You look like a school girl at her first dance.

CATHERINE : M'enfin. Il est assez jeune pour être mon fils. C'est absurde ce que tu dis.

MARY: It's not true he's young enough to be your son. But he's old enough to be your lover.

CATHERINE : *(Elle s'assied sur un banc. Elle écoute le bruit des canons. [She sits on a bench. She listens to the sound of the cannons.])* C'est si évident que ça?

MARY: Yes, it is. And I am only telling you because I am your dear friend and care about you.

CATHERINE : Tu m'en veux d'être amoureuse d'un jeune homme?

MARY: No. I don't hold it against you. None of us are saints, even the ones who pretend to be.

CATHERINE : Pierre est si souvent parti depuis des années. Il semble être toujours d'une plantation à l'autre. Toujours les affaires. Toujours les absences. Je déteste être seule, Marie.

MARY: And Pierre is alone, too, isn't he?

CATHERINE : Non. Il a ces maîtresses de couleur comme tous les autres. Je sais très bien qu'il a acheté une maisonnette Rue Bayonne pour une des ces maîtresses. Au sujet des autres, je n'en sais rien de précis, mais je suis certaine qu'il en a eu d'autres.

MARY: He's just a man, like all the others. Never enough with one woman. And Louis, what is he really like?

CATHERINE : Il est si beau, si jeune, si intentionné. Il a tellement souffert avant de quitter Port-au-Prince. Il a sauvé beaucoup de gens avant de s'enfuir lui-même. J'admire tellement son courage, son esprit, son enthousiasme.

MARY: I must confess that I have feelings for John's nephew, Christopher. He's such a remarkable young man.

CATHERINE : Vous êtes amants?

MARY: No. But sometimes I imagine it. Even that makes me feel so guilty. I thought I was a modern, emancipated woman, but even thinking of Christopher makes me feel weak and unfaithful, even dirty somehow.

CATHERINE : (Elles prends les mains de MARY. [She takes MARY's hands.]) Non. Les pensées d'amour ne sont jamais sales. Jamais.

MARY: And what if Pierre or John gets killed in the fighting?

CATHERINE : Ou Louis, ou Christopher?

MARY: God forbid! *(Elles restent en silence. [They remain in silence.])* Listen?

CATHERINE : Quoi? Je n'entends plus rien.

MARY: That's it. There isn't any more shelling.

CATHERINE : Ecoute. Les chevaux arrivent.

MARY: Do Pierre and John know where we're waiting?

CATHERINE : Oui.

> *PIERRE et JOHN entrent. Tous les deux portent des bandages tachés du sang. Leurs vêtements sont sales et déchirés. Les femmes s'approchent de leurs maris pour les aider. Ils s'embrassent. (PIERRE and JOHN enter. They both are wearing blood-stained bandages. Their clothing is dirty and torn. The woman rush to help their husbands. They embrace.)*

MARY: Thank God you're alive. And the British are they coming?

JOHN: Completed defeated. We are victorious. General Jackson, Laffite, the townspeople, the colored, Creoles and Americans everyone fought side by side and we won. The British lost thousands and we only lost a few hundred. It was unbelievable.

CATHERINE : Que Dieu soit loué. Et Louis, comment va-t-il?

PIERRE : Il vit, mais il est gravement blessé.

CATHERINE : Gravement? Il risque de mourir?

PIERRE : Non. Je crois qu'il vivra.

MARY: And Christopher?

JOHN: He died, shot through the heart in the first few minutes of fighting. He died a hero's death, Mary.

MARY : *(Elle s'asseid sur le banc et commence à pleurer. [She sits on the bench and starts to cry.])* My God, so young.

JOHN: Young and already a hero. He died saving New Orleans. His father will be so proud of him.

MARY: And his mother, will she be proud, too?

JOHN: Of course. It was a great victory. What mother would not be happy to have her son die a hero in a great victory?

MARY: Of course, a great victory.

PIERRE : C'est vrai, Marie. J'ai tout vu. Il est tombé avec une balle dans sa poitrine. Il n'a même pas eu le temps de souffrir. C'est comme ça qu'il aurait voulu sa mort. C'était magnifique à voir, un jeune homme qui combattait comme un lion pour défendre son pays contre des agresseurs. Il était comme un soldat dans la Grande Armée de Napoléon. Oui, un héros dans n'importe quelle langue.

MARY: Napoleon, Napoleon and still Napoleon. We are Americans now. We are one people whether we speak French or English. I don't want to hear anything more about that monster. His filthy European wars are the root of this invasion. Your Napoleon is a monster.

PIERRE : *(Il s'assied à côté d'elle et met le bras autour de l'épaule de MARY. [He sits next next to MARY and puts his arm around her.])* Il n'est pas un monstre. Et peut-être un jour il sera notre empereur de nouveau.

MARY: You live in the past, you deluded, pathetic fool.

JOHN: Mary! Stop this at once. We just fought a tremendous battle and saved New Orleans from the British. Everyone came together, Creoles,

Americans, rich, poor, black, white, priests and pirates. It was beautiful victory, a great victory for everyone. Please, I know you're upset about Christopher, but don't spoil it for us and certainly don't insult our dear friend.

MARY: I'm sorry. I got carried away. *(A PIERRE. [To PIERRE.])* Please excuse me, Pierre. We both value your friendship.

PIERRE : Je comprends ta douleur. Je sais que tu souffres pour ton neveu. Nous avons tous souffert. Mais maintenant il faut bénéficier des fruits de notre grande victoire. Je t'en pris, ma chère Marie.

MARY: I'm sorry. I'm upset. I have been insensitive to your efforts, to your sacrifices. Please forgive me, Pierre.

PIERRE : Bien sûr. Je t'excuse. Mais je ne peux pas oublier que c'est sur les cadavres des nous ancêtres et nos compatriotes que notre colonie a été fondée. C'est sur les ossement de ces héros que notre Louisiane a été construite. Je regarde vers le futur, et non pas vers le passé. Je crois au futur, Marie. Catherine et moi admirons encore notre Empereur et nous l'aiderons si nous le pouvons. Mais nous sommes maintenant les Américains et notre obligation et envers notre nouveau pays, les Etats-Unis d'Amérique.

CATHERINE : Viens Marie. Allons priez pour les morts et les blessés. Laissez nos hommes répandre les bonnes nouvelles partout dans la ville. *(Les femmes commence à sortir. Les cloches commencent à sonner joyeusement. [The women begin to leave. Bells begin to ring joyously.])*

PIERRE : Pas la peine pour nous de répandre les nouvelles. Les cloches de la cathédrale St. Louis sonnent déjà. Toute la ville est au courant maintenant. Nous n'avons qu'à rentrer chez nous pour nous laver.

JOHN: President Madison will know of this great victory soon enough. Let's hope that General Jackson himself will take the news back to Washington.

MARY: Leave the details to the generals. You have both done your duty. Christopher has done his as well. We have all sacrificed enough.

PIERRE : *(Il s'apprête à partir. [They begin to leave.])* D'abord je dois aller communiquer les nouvelles à un ami, Rue Bayonne. Il sera très content de connaître se qui s'est passé.

CATHERINE : Pourquoi il? Elle est sûrement au courant de la victoire, mais peut-être pas encore du fait que tu aies survécu à la bataille.

PIERRE : Elle?

CATHERINE : Victoire ou non, je sais que ta maîtresse quarteronne est la personne que tu veux rencontrer là-bas. S'il te plaît, Pierre, assez de mensonges. Peut-être faut-il fêter notre grande victoire avec un peu d'honnêteté. Tu ne trouves pas?

JOHN: Let's leave you two alone. I think you need some privacy.

CATHERINE : Non! J'ai honte de l'admettre mais j'ai presque voulu que tu sois tué au camp de bataille, Pierre, et non pas le cousin de John. C'est triste à dire, mais c'est la vérité.

PIERRE : Et toi? Ton Louis? J'aurai dû lui tirer dans le dos moi-même. Malheureusement, les anglais l'ont seulement touché au bras. Seulement le bras et pas le cœur où il le méritait. Tu crois vraiment que je suis aussi aveugle que ça?

CATHERINE : Oui, tu dois être aveugle. Parce qu'apparemment tu n'as pas remarqué qu'il est blanc au moins. Pas comme ta putain quarteronne.

PIERRE : *(Il avance sur CATHERINE, le bras levé pour la frapper. [He advances on CATHERINE with his arm raised to strike her.])* Salope!

JOHN : *(Il se place entre les époux. [He places himself between the couple.])* No! *(Il prend le bras de PIERRE. [He takes PIERRE's arm.])* No man strikes a woman, especially their own wife.

PIERRE : Elle doit être punie pour son insolence.

CATHERINE : Oui, comme tes autres esclaves!

PIERRE : Comment oses-tu! *(Il avance de nouveau. [He advances again.])*

CATHERINE : J'ose parce que je ne suis pas ton esclave, même si tu me considère comme tel.

JOHN : *(Il attrape PIERRE et le jette par terre. [He takes PIERRE and throws him to the ground.])* Leave her!

CATHERINE : Laisse-le venir. Au moins tout le monde saura comment le grand héros de guerre Monsieur Pierre traite sa femme.

PIERRE : Pourquoi veux-tu tout gâcher? Pourquoi insistes-tu pour dénigrer par tes accusations tout ce que nous avons accompli ce jour?

MARY : *(Elle s'approche de PIERRE pour l'aider à se mettre debout. [She goes to take PIERRE to help him stand up.])* You are a hero, Pierre. And so are John and Louis. But your wife needs you too, not just your country. You need each other. No one thinks you are perfect. You both have your needs, your hopes, and your disappointments. But it's time to put them aside, to start afresh. Build something new and strong, something better. Let's go to our homes and thank God for what has happened today, everything. It all must be the will of God.

JOHN: And what about Christopher? Shouldn't we help with his funeral preparations?

MARY: Let his own family take care of him. They will have enough grief without our adding to it with our presence. Today we cherish the living, let's wait to bury the dead. *(Elle prend JOHN par le bras. PIERRE fait de même avec CATHERINE et ils sortent tous. [She takes JOHN by the bras. PIERRE does the same with CATHERINE and they all leave.])*

ACT III (April 30, 1832)

Act III takes place in the home of MARY and JOHN. The room is a parlor with several chairs and a small couch. It is decorated in the American Style, with Queen Anne type furniture, perhaps an oriental rug.
(L'Acte III se passe dans la maison de MARY et JOHN. La pièce est un salon avec plusieurs fauteuils et un petit divan. C'est décoré dans le Style Américain avec les meubles Reine Anne et peut-être un tapis d'orient.)

MARY: Come in, come in! *(PIERRE and CATHERINE enter.)*

JOHN: Welcome to you both. *(He kisses CATHERINE on each cheek in the French fashion and shakes hands with PIERRE.)* So glad you could join us for this little celebration.

PIERRE: The pleasure is ours. You are always such gracious hosts.

CATHERINE: *(She hugs MARY.)* Your new home is so lovely. My compliments.

MARY: Thank you so much. Come in. Sit down. *(PIERRE and CATHERINE sit on the couch and JOHN sits in a chair. Mary goes out and returns with a tray with a bottle of champagne and four glasses.)* And here is something special for a special occasion.

JOHN: Special indeed. What can be more special than the twentieth anniversary of Louisiana's statehood? My heavens, 1812 to 1832, does it seem possible? Twenty years gone by and it seems like a moment in time.

ALL: (*They take their glasses and stand up. They click their glasses together*)
To the state of Louisiana!

JOHN: This has really been an astonishing twenty years. So much change, so much progress.

PIERRE: Yes, change indeed. We are now a city of 100,000. French is heard in whispers and down dark alleys in the Vieux Carré. English is everywhere and soon we Creoles will be a memory. There has been progress, but much has been lost and much will still be lost.

JOHN: Come now, Pierre. It hasn't been all bad. Your businesses are booming and so are mine. Perhaps one door has closed, but others are opening every day.

CATHERINE: Indeed. Many doors have opened to prostitutes, unscrupulous businessmen, protestant clergy, Jews, and all sorts of riff-raff from every corner of Europe except France. We only have one French bookstore left, and one newspaper. The French Opera is always losing money. The Académie des Soeurs Du Sacré Coeur has closed. No one but Gayarre is keeping the Société Française alive, and it has been reduced to a shadow of its former self. My God, all you hear around here is English, English, and English with some German and Italian thrown in. It's shameful.

PIERRE: She is right, you know. From France to Spain to France to the United States. I'm afraid our dear Louisiana has been through quite a journey. And I'm afraid it's not over. Did you hear the abolitionist rumblings from the North? New England never wanted us to be a state from the beginning and now they are doing everything to support the elimination of slavery. What will my plantations be like without labor? I could never pay the taxes, much less make a profit with hired help. A good slave already costs hundreds and they die like flies from every attack of yellow fever. It's hardly even viable economically. Maybe the Northerners are right. Maybe it is time to be done with the whole system of slavery?

CATHERINE: And now who is the revolutionary? Ending slavery. Ending our way of life. Have you become so dangerously radical now?

PIERRE: Maybe I have become more revolutionary in my old days. I have been wrong in the past, so perhaps I have been wrong again, wrong to keep hanging on to a life that is already passing us by. Things have changed in ways we would never have dreamed of a few decades ago. We Creoles were the undisputed masters of this strange land. And now it is another country and we are just old people holding on to old ways that are doomed. First French will go, then slavery. Mark my words.

CATHERINE: I already miss the grand balls, the glittering opera. Do you remember that magnificent performance of Don Juan at the Opéra Française a few years ago?

PIERRE: Yes, of course. With the real flames that shot up from the stage. It was spectacular.

MARY: I remember. Women fainted.

CATHERINE: And the heat from the flames nearly burned the place down. My heavens, what a wonderful evening.

PIERRE: Now they can't even fill that place half way for any performance.

JOHN: They should close the Opéra Française down anyway. It should have closed ten years ago when it ceased making money. Who is going to pay to keep it open? The City Council? The Société Française? They hardly have enough members now to keep that going. *L'Abeille* only prints a few thousand copies of their French language newspaper for a city of a hundred thousand. That should tell you something. It's all past. French is a thing of the past, and so are the duels and the quadroon balls. Now we have street lights and decent sewage and honest government. We are on the way to a glorious future as an important state in the Union where English will reign supreme from coast to coast, from the borders of Canada to the borders of Mexico.

PIERRE: Yes, we Creoles are people of the past. And we can honor that past, or at least we should. Every bayou, every little town, and many street names are French and those names will honor our ancestors even when we are all dead and gone. French will linger here like the smell of coffee. (*He pauses.*) And I am not convinced that your English speaking future will be so glorious. This Union may be built on sand and we may all be swept away by terrible winds from the North.

JOHN: Don't be so gloomy. Business is booming, the city is booming. Life is good even if we only speak in English.

PIERRE: Are you ashamed to speak French now? Even to old friends like us.

JOHN: No, of course not. But we have decided not to speak French in our home so the children will not have an inappropriate accent for their future.

CATHERINE: No French for the children?

MARY: No, no French. It was a mutual decision that John and I made some time ago.

PIERRE: What a pity.

JOHN: It's not a pity, Pierre. It's progress. Like everything that has been happening here for the last twenty years.

PIERRE: Progress? Theaters closing? Bookstores closing? Fine Free Men of Color treated like they were humble slaves. No gentility. No pretense of education or refinement.

JOHN: Pierre! That notion of superior Creole gentility and education is nothing by a myth fostered on us by old Gayarre from the Société Française. Gentility? Education? Just lies. At least now public schools are open for the lower classes, not just for the very rich. Maybe it's not in French. And maybe there's no Latin and Greek, but even poor children can learn to read and write. I can give you the names of all the intelligent and educated Creoles and you are, indeed, among them. But what about the rest, the French speaking workers and shop keepers with barely enough education to keep their books? There's no pride in that. They are no better than our poor white trash who put on airs of superiority over the blacks and the Italian and German immigrants.

MARY: Pierre and Catherine are still our honored guest. Please treat them as such. I forbid you from continuing this diatribe. Have some charity. We all helped build this town together. Now don't drive them away from our home by your mean-spiritedness. Our friendship has covered decades and will hopefully cover decades more.

PIERRE: We are already old. I doubt we can live too many more decades. And with us, so dies a way of life.

CATHERINE: I would like to propose another toast. *(She raises her glass and the others follow.)* To friendship, regardless of the language, regardless of the age!

ALL: To friendship! *(They click their glasses and drink. The music of a polka comes in from the wings.)*

PIERRE: To our new French-speaking governor, André Bienville Roman! Perhaps the last native French speaker we'll have.

ALL: To Governor Roman!

MARY: Listen. It's that new dance from Eastern Europe, from Bohemia, the polka.

CATHERINE: The polka? Do you know how it goes?

MARY: Yes. I learned it from Louis. I believe that I see him more often then you do, for my dance lessons.

CATHERINE: No doubt you do. I am too matronly now to think of such things as young men and dancing.

MARY : You do yourself a disservice, Catherine. Louis still thinks and speaks kindly of you.

CATHERINE: That's nice of you to say. But at my age, I should be thinking of more spiritual things. In fact, I have approached the mother superior at the Ursuline Convent to discuss my entry into their order should something happen to Pierre.

MARY: (She laughs.) I should think if something happens to Pierre or John, then we should both move into the Baroness Pontabla's apartments on Jackson Square and lead a life of dissipation among the last of the Creoles, don't you?

PIERRE: You two have already buried us and we are very much alive. Now how about this new dance? Perhaps you can show it to us. I think I need to kick up these aging legs before my wife buries us both alive.

MARY: (She gets up, lifts up her skirt, and begins). They say the polka comes from Bohemia and it goes like this: left-two-three, hop, right-two-three hop, left-two-three, hop and keep repeating. It's the rage all over Europe. Let's try.

JOHN: Not another dance. You've gone crazy since you've started taking dance lessons. This Louis is definitely a bad influence.

MARY: (She drags JOHN up and they assume the dance position.) Yes, dear, the worst imaginable. And you are going to learn another dance. Now, let's try. (They dance the polka to some lively music.) Now it's your turn, Catherine and Pierre.

CATHERINE: (She grabs PIERRE and pulls him up.) Come on, old man. We don't want to live in the past, do we? Let's dance our way into the future.

(The music gets louder and the couples dance an animated polka as the lights dim to dark.)

FIN-THE END

NEPŮJDU Z HOSPODY
(I WON'T LEAVE THE PUB)

(Translated by Josef Hoch,

and Alena Adamikova)

POSTAVY:

JARMILA KOSTEL: Pozdní čtyřicátnice až ranná padesátnice.. Zdá se být lehce plnoštíhlá a má nepatrný přízvuk jižní oblasti.

KAREL KOSTEL: Padesátník. On má také venkovský akcent bez jakéhokoliv českého přízvuku.

MÍSTO:

Dům Jarmily a Karla Kostelových v Libuši, Louisiana.

DĚJOVÁ LINIE: Jarmila se snaží naučit Karla nějaké kroky českého tance pro nadcházející český festival. On chce vzdát tančení, které vede ke slovní hádce s jeho chotí.

Scéna obsahuje stůl a pár jednoduchých židlí s malým ohybem nechávajíc větší část jeviště na tančení. Na stole je malý, přenosný CD přehrávač.

JARMILA: *(Světla provázejí Jarmilu a Karla, zvedají ruce jeden druhého do vzduchu levou za pravou. Snaží se ji otočit a udělat okno, ale beznadějně se zamotají. Jarmila zakopává o Karlovu nohu a padá.)* Ne! Ne! Ne! Takhle ne Karle. Musíš mě nechat otočit se pod tvými pažemi.

KAREL: *(Pouští nespokojeně Jarmiliny ruce.)* For God's sake, Jarmilo. To je těžká figura dostat se doprava.

JARMILA: Já vím drahý. Nakonec to bude vypadat skvěle, když se přes to přeneseme. Teď uchop moji pravou ruku za tvojí pravou ruku. A uchop moji levou ruku s tvojí. . .za pravou. Zvedni svoje paže. A nech mě otočit se pod tebou.

KAREL: *(On to zkouší znovu. Dostávají se lehce dál, potom se zamotají a znovu zastaví.)* Tohle nemůžu dělat! Můžeme se zastavit a udělat si alespoň malou přestávku? Ty mě s tím zabíjíš.

JARMILA: Dobře.Udělejme si malou přestávku.Donesu dvě piva. V pořádku? *(On přikývne hlavou a ona mizí ze scény a objevuje se s dvěma plzeňskými pivy. Podá jedno Karlovi a oba se posadí a dají si pořádný hlt.)*

KAREL: Díky.To jsem potřeboval.

JARMILA: To pivo je dobré, že?

KAREL: Jo.O hodně lepší než naše tančení. *(On se znovu napije.)* Drahoušku, opravdu chceš pokračovat v tomto českém tančení?

JARMILA: Myslíš dnes?

KAREL: Ne Myslím celkově.Opravdu chceš pokračovat ve folklórním tanci?

JARMILA: Pokračovat v tančení! Co je to za hloupou otázku. Samozřejmě, že chci pokračovat v tančení. Já ráda tančím. Když se obleču do mého kroje, cítím se výjimečná, krásná. Já vím,že nejsem tak krásná, ale v tom kroji se cítím krásná.Kromě toho, je to naše tradice,naše kultura.

KAREL: Já vím. Ale nepřipadá mi, že se někdy můžu přenést přes tyto tance.

JARMILA: Tyto tance pocházejí přímo ze starého světa, přímo ze středu Evropy do středu Lousiany. Jsou naše cenná tradice.

KAREL: *(Usrkává piva a dívá se do láhve.)*Plzeňské pivo. Toto je část naší cenné tradice, kterou umím ocenit. Ostatně nikdo z nás nemluví česky.Jenom hrstka starých lidí okolo stále mluví. A všechno tohle tančení a kostýmová stafáž, to je jen šaráda.Všechno je to vytvořené Jarmilo.

JARMILLA: To není!Naše kroje pocházejí z Čech a Moravy.My jsme je okopírovali podle pravých, tamních originálů .

KAREL: Jo, originály, které přivezli Parkerovi ze svých cest. Je to jen kopírování, jako Disney World, padělek české vesnice právě tady ve střední Louisianě. Jistě, je to opravdu pěkné, ale stačí jen uvěřit.

JARMILA: Ale tance jsou pravé odtud a ty to víš.

KAREL: Jo. Také přivezeny ze starého světa od Parkerů. Hele, Jarmilo, jediné tance našich rodičů,které tady stále tančili byly waltz a polka, ne všechny ty zábavné, folklórní tance, které nás Parkerovi naučili.

JARMILA: Karle, nebudu se bavit o Parkerových. Kromě toho, jestli se nechceš učit o své kultuře kvůli sobě, nebo kvůli mne, tak co hledisko tvého syna, Petra.

KAREL: Petr? Co mu na tom záleží? On se jen veze a dělá co děláme my. Myslíš si,že se opravdu zajímá o některou z těchto folklórní věcí? Tance? Kroje?

JARMILA: Ano myslím. Myslím si, že mu to dává důležitý vědomí místa, kulturní identity.

KAREL: Dobře, možná máš pravdu, ale zaměstnává ho to nějak? Potřebuje zaměstnání Jarmilo. Potřebuje dobře placenou práci a místo sám pro sebe. To je to co potřebuje, ne nedůležité folklórní tance a původní etnické kroje.

JARMILA: Ty ale dokážeš být nespravedlivý. Petr se snažil najít práci po měsíce. Tady venku nic není. A taky bere hodiny.

KAREL: Takže my stále platíme účty a on se učí jak tančit české folklórní tance pro dobro jeho kulturní sebeúcty. To je úžasný plán. Kromě toho je tu spousta práce. Možná se jen necítí kvalifikovaný.

JARMILA: To není pravda. Žádal všude a nebyl přijat. Jako v papírně.

KAREL: Nikdy nežádal v papírně. Mluvil jsem tam s Frank Beaumontem. Petr se nikdy neukázal, když sháněli zájemce.

JARMILA: Ale on mi řekl že nebyl prostě přijat.

KAREL: On nežádal. Věř mi nebo ne. Nikdy se nešel tam zeptat.

JARMILA: Ale proč?

KAREL: Zeptej se jeho. Možná, že byl příliš unavený z toho všeho folklórního tancování?

JARMILA: *(Napřímila se a vyzvala svého manžela.)*Dost kecání. Myslím, že se musíme vrátit ke cvičení.S takovým tempem nikdy nebudeme připraveni na český festival. Ty potřebuješ cvičit. Nestihl si dost nácviků tak jako tak.

KAREL: Já jsem snad pracoval drahoušku. Nemůžu všechno na staveništi zahodit a říct mému šéfovi, že končím s odléváním cementu a odcházím tančit folklórní tance. *(Sám se zvedá. A vrací se do jejich pozice s levou rukou přes pravou. On zvedá paže a ona se kroutí pod nimi. Utvoří figuru okna a začínají se otáčet a potom se snaží uvolnit ze zamotané pozice.)* Sakra! Zapomeň na tuto kravinu. Je mi z toho špatně.

JARMILA: Neodvažuj se to vzdát takhle, Karle Kostele!

KAREL: *(Svalil se a znovu se chopil svého piva.)*Vzdávám to Jarmilo. Je mi z tohoto tance špatně. Ve skutečnosti je mi špatně z celé této hovadiny. Je mi špatně z mých kámošů volající na mě teplouši kvůli mé opeřené čepici a lemované vestě. *(Napodobuje jiného muže, který ho zesměšňuje.)* Jé Karle. Vypadáš tak roztomile v té malé, rozkošné čepici. A točíš se a kroutíš se jako opravdová balerína. *(Vrací se ke svému normálnímu hlasu.)* Myslíš si, že rád slyším ty voloviny znovu a znovu? Kvůli čemu? Kvůli folklóru? Kvůli mému českému dědictví? Tomu čelím již léta. Jarmilo. Vyhov mně a nech mě to vzdát.. To je tvoje věc, ne moje. To je Parkerových věc, ne moje. Pokračuj a tancuj jestli chceš, jestli ti nevadí tancovat s tvým vlastním synem. *(Dopíjí pivo a praští s lahví.)* Končím s touto hovadinou. Vzdávám to.

JARMILA: *(Ona se posadí a studuje Karla.)*Jaký druh sdělení si myslíš, že zanecháváš svému synovi?

KAREL: Že se nerad oblékám jako klaun a tancuju dokola jako teplouš. Že nemám rád své přátele a spolupracovníky a dokonce členy mojí vlastní rodiny dělající si ze mě srandu. Radši bych venku lovil nebo rybařil.A co o tom sdělení? Je to opravdu tak špatné sdělení sdělit ho vlastnímu synovi?

JARMILA: To není špatné poselství. Ale nemyslím si, že je to poselství, které mu posíláš.

KAREL: Potom jaké poselství myslíš, že mu posílám?

JARMILA: Myslím, že mu zanecháváš poselství, že když je něco těžké nebo jiné nebo, když si z tebe lidi dělají srandu, pak to vzdáš.

KAREL: To je blbost a ty to víš! Jestli se učím folklórní tance nebo ne, je to úplně jedno Petrovi.

JARMILA: Možná.Možná ne. Ale chceš, aby se vykašlal na věci, které jsou trochu obtížnější? Chceš, aby se vzdal, když ho lidi kritizují nebo, když si z něj dělají srandu? Chceš, aby říkal, že žádá o práci a potom nechodil na všechny pohovory?

KAREL: Přeháníš Jarmilo a ty to víš.

JARMILA: Možná. Ale jen o tom přemýšlej. Vzdal někdy něco tvůj otec?

KAREL: Samozřejmě, že ne. Dřel jako pes. Pracoval skrz bídu. Snesl to, že všichni v městě ho nazývali kolohnátem.. Sbíral zemáky až mu krvácely ruce. Ten muž pracoval a pracoval nikdy nic nevzdal. Potom hurikánu co tu udeřil pomohl přestavět ten český sál a nikdy nechtěl groš za svůj čas nebo svoje dříví. Ten muž byl svatý a neodvažuj se říct o něm něco špatného.

JARMILA: Neříkám nic špatného Karle. Já poukazuju na to, že tvůj syn se bude dívat na tebe stejným způsobem. A bude očekávat stejné chování.

KAREL: Pro pána boha ! Jak můžeš srovnávat nějaké hloupé tančení s bojem o přežití v době ekonomické krize a muset snášet ty mizerné místní snoby?

JARMILA: Oba jsou ponaučením v životě, že? Zachovaná kultura. Přenášející se na tvoje děti.

KAREL: Nebuď praštěná Jarmilo. Vstávám každé ráno a chodím do práce a potom o víkendech pracuju tady okolo. Pomáhám strýci Fredovi s jeho zatracenýma bramborama a strýci Harveyovi s jeho dřevem.Moje ruce, moje kolena, moje záda, všechno mě bolí z té nucené práce. Ale nad hlavou máme střechu a na stole jídlo. Není právě etická ta práce, která se má předávat dál? Ne tenhle falešný, kulturní nesmysl. (*Odmlčí se.*) Tatínek chodil tančit. On věděl jak tančit waltz a polku. Ale nikdy v životě neslyšel o těchto vyumělkovaných krocích. Nikdy si neoblíkal příšerný klobouk a zdobené vesty. Ten chlap nikdy nevyšel bez svých montérek. Ale mluvil česky, a říct toto o nás já nemůžu. .

JARMILA: Tohle všechno je pravda. A byl dobrý muž, skvělý muž. Ale on by byl na tebe pyšný v tvém příšerném klobouku a pěkné vestě. On by byl prasknul pýchou vidět tě točit se dokola a učit svého syna dělat totéž.A neříkej, že neumíš mluvit česky.

KAREL: Ale jdi! Říkat *pivo* a *kolače neplatí.* .

JARMILA: Proč ne Možná tyhle taneční záležitosti jsou lehčí než učit se česky. Tvůj tatínek neměl příležitost naučit se ji. Myslím si, že by to měl rád. A jak jsi řekl, on nikdy nic nevzdal a ty bys neměl taky.

KAREL: *(Napije se z prázdné láhve.)*Jo, on byl skoro svatý. Ale něčeho se přece vzdal.

JARMILA: Co?

KAREL: Když dokončil střední školu, mluvil o chození na střední školu, na lesnickou. Ale vzdal tu myšlenku, aby mohl zůstat a pracovat na farmě.

JARMILA: To nebyla jeho chyba.To byla krize. Byl to strašný čas. Nikdo neměl peníze jít na školu.Všichni museli pracovat, aby se uživili.

KAREL: To je pravda.Ale když jsem dokončil střední školu mluvil jsem s ním o odchodu na školu, možná na strojařinu.Vždycky jsem byl docela dobrý na matiku.A on jen poslouchal. Nikdy nic neřekl.

JARMILA: Ale to byla tvoje volba nejít študovat, ne jeho.

KAREL: Já vím. Ale s malým tlakem, s malým povzbuzením.Myslím, že jsem to měl zkusit Jarmilo. A kdo ví kde bych byl nebo jak bych si teď žil? *(Odmlčí se.)* Já jsem jen potřeboval trochu postrčit. Myslím si, že jsem mohl dostat stipendium, o létech bych pracoval.Podívej se na mě teď Jarmilo, jsem jen manuální dělník, celý den liju beton. Podívej se na moje ruce, hrubé a šupinaté,pokryté mozoly.

JARMILA: *(Pohybuje se napříč a bere jeho ruce.)*Tvoje ruce jsou nádherné Karle. Ty jsou první věc, které jsem si na tobě všimla.

KAREL: Ne můj pohledný obličej?

JARMILA: Ne. Ne tvůj pohledný obličej. Tvé silné ruce. Líbili se mi jak vypadají a jejich cit. A pořád se mi líbí. Ony jsou ruce pravého muže. *(Pokládá si je na svůj obličej.)* Je to v pořádku jestli nechceš pokračovat v tančení. Nemusíš. A Petr může nebo nemusí pokračovat jestli nechceš. Ale on tě bude stále obdivovat ať budeš tančit nebo ne. Vím, že bude. A já budu taky.

Kromě toho, vždycky můžu tančit s tvým bratrancem Harrym. On je dobrý tanečník s dobrou pamětí pro tanec a také s velkými rukama.

KAREL Silné ruce! Jistě. Silné dost na bití jeho první i druhé ženy. To je pěkná síla!.

JARMILA: Ale on miluje tanec. Chytne mě ve svém stisku a jen mě točí dokola jako káču. Je to trochu opojné, víš jak , jako silné pití po horkém dni v práci.Možná, že není taková milá osoba, ale je velmi dobrý tanečník. A taky nevypadá špatně. Nesouhlasíš?

KAREL: *(Karel si povzdechne a zamračí se.)*Dobře. Vynechejme z toho Harryho. Jsem ochotný dát tomuto tanci ještě příležitost. Samozřejmě kvůli Petrovi. Tak, můžeme zkusit jen tu otáčecí část?

JARMILA: Levé ruce za pravé. Zvedni paže. *(Ona se podtočí a udělají okno. Jak obkrouží dokola, dívají se velmi upřeně jeden na druhého. Karel ji roztočí.)* Teď se obrátím a zatímco půjdu pozpátku ty uděláš tvůj krok plácání boty.

KAREL: *(Tleská jeho rukama, potom plácá jeho zdviženou, pravou nohou, potom to opakuje s levou nohou. Následně udělá tři rychlé vpravo-vlevo-vpravo tlesky na svoje stehna, plácne svým pravým, zdviženým chodidlem. Zopakuje to s jeho levým, zdviženým chodidlem.)*Dobrý Bože. Myslím, že je to správně.

JARMILA: To bylo správně Karle! Bylo to perfektní! Jsi připravený zkusit to s hudbou?

KAREL: Myslíš si,že jsme připraveni?

JARMILA: Ne zcela. Musíme se dostat do správné vnitřní nálady. Teď se na mě podívej a představ si mě oblečenou v mojí bílé blůze s načechranými rukávy a v moji červeno-zelené, vyšívané vestě.

KAREL: Tu jak se Ti tlačí kozy ven?

JARMILA: Ano, právě tu, ale ta prsní část je volitelná. Teď si představ moji bílou sukni, všechno vzdouvající se. A moji tištěnou, modrou zástěru a černé, lesklé boty. Máš tu vnitřní představu?

KAREL: Mám to všechno.

JARMILA: Teď si představ sebe vysoce stojícího se svým skvělým černým kloboukem, celý dekorovaný peřím a lemy a tvoji červenou vestu s modrou obrubou, kterou jsem vyšívala steh po stehu. A tvoji košili s výšivkou, kterou pro tebe ušila teta Helena.

KAREL: Ta na kterou jsem vylil kečup na minulém českém festivalu?

JARMILA: Ano, tamtu, ale bez té kečupové části. Dobře, jak vypadáme?

KAREL: Nevím jak já, ale ty vypadáš překrásně.

JARMILA: Lacině a falešně?

KAREL: Ne. Vypadáš tak opravdově Jarmilo. Česká princezna. Vypadáš jako samotná kněžna Libuše. *(Líbá ji.)* Moje krásná, česká princezna. Teď můžeme začít.

JARMILA: *(Směje se a líbá jeho ruce.)*Můj pohledný český princ se svýma silnýma rukama. *(Potom ona přechází a pouští malý CD přehrávač.)* Pojďme. *(Hudbou je český tanec „Nepujdu z Hospody (I Won't leave the Pub)." Choreografie je od Evy a Radka Rejskových. Tanec trvá 1 minutu 43 sekund, ale je třeba použít polovinu s kroky z druhé části tance. Ta část obsahuje pohyb okno a dupání botami. Hudba by měla být zcela nahlas. Pár tančí bezchybně a světla se rychle ztlumí do tmy jak Karel skončí s posledním dupnutím boty.)*

ABOUT THE AUTHOR

David J. Holcombe was born in San Francisco and raised in the East Bay Area in the shadow of Mount Diablo. He received a BSA from the University of California at Davis, followed by a MSA from the University of Florida, and a MD from the Catholic University of Louvain in Brussels, Belgium. After working 20 years as an internist in Alexandria, Louisiana, he switched his orientation and continued his medical career in public health. During his many academic and professional years, he continued to write short stories and plays. He has published two collections of short stories, *"Like Honored and Trusted Colleagues"* and *"Cappuccino at Podgorica."* This collection of short plays, *"Beauty and the Botox,"* compliments his short stories and explores themes of human nature and social folly. He currently lives with his wife in Central Louisiana, where they participate in the cultural and social life of the city and state.